Lives & Loves of

LETTON HALL

Norfolk

Published by Jigsaw Design & Publishing, Norwich

Every effort has been made to trace copyright holders and to obtain their permission for the use of copyright material. The publisher apologises for any errors or omissions and would be grateful if notified of any corrections that should be incorporated in future reprints or editions of this book.

Designed and produced by Jigsaw Design & Publishing. www.jigsaw-publishing.co.uk
Printed in Great Britain by Swallowtail Print
11050-1/11
ISBN 978-1-907750-33-5

Lives & Loves of
LETTON HALL
Norfolk

THE BIOGRAPHY OF SIR JOHN SOANE'S FIRST HOUSE

Peter Carroll

To my patient and supportive family

ACKNOWLEDGEMENTS

In compiling the earlier chapters I am grateful for the expert assistance given to me by Sir John Soane's Museum, the Norfolk Record Office, the Norfolk County Council Museums and Historic Environment Service, and the Centre of East Anglian Studies at the University of East Anglia.

I am also particularly grateful for the kindness of Lord Cranworth in allowing me access to the relevant sections of the Gurdon family papers and portraits.

The later chapters are within living memory and, having spent more than 25 years collecting information, listening to stories, and following up and researching leads, there are very many people whose help I need to acknowledge. I hope I have done this in the text, notes and captions, but if I have missed out any key names, or recorded facts inaccurately, then I sincerely apologise.

In addition to those already acknowledged, I am grateful for the photographic assistance of Tim Baldwin, Jack Carroll, Dave Ham, Roger D Fenton and others who have kindly loaned me snapshots and family albums.

Front cover: Picture of Letton Hall viewed from the north east, used by kind permission of Ptolemy Dean.

CONTENTS

PREFACE

Letton Hall is an important house architecturally but many books have been written about far finer houses by experts far better qualified than I. My motives in writing are not merely for academic record but are rather more personal.

After owning the house for 30 years I came to love it; it came to life for me, and I for it. One doesn't so much 'own' a house like Letton, but it's more a matter of 'living together': I may have been master, but the house was mistress; I may have been the squire but I was also its slave.

It is a living relationship that defies an easy summary, but I suspect many others have felt it over the years. Many lives have been lived at Letton and the building has had an affect on them; it has marked changes in their circumstances, and they have left their mark on the building – and it is this relationship between Letton and its occupants that I seek to capture, and so bring the house alive to readers.

In a 250-year life Letton has witnessed much love and a lot of loss. The architecture is inextricably linked with those who have dwelt at Letton and it is this touch of walls steeped in history, and the sense of so many people having been here before, living their lives before me, that brought the past alive. I can still thrill to the opening of a door that reveals one of John Soane's vistas or axes, even after 30 years of doing so; and I can take in the fascination of the staircase, or enjoy the proportions of an arched window, and still feel a glow of appreciation.

In writing this book there is also the practical aim of making a record. Time moves on relentlessly and although much historical material is in safe keeping, a lot of the ephemera blows by; photographs are handed down to the next generation without a key, and anecdotes and names are forgotten… so I have had a sense of urgency in trying to capture the moment, and hope to have provided an opportunity for other people to make their contributions. There is a moment when one reaches the end of the archives and the beginning of the anecdotes.

The arrangement of the book is more-or-less chronological. '*There is properly no history; only biographies*' said Ralph Waldo Emerson, and the history of a house must be mainly the history of the people living in it. So as the people progress through the generations and the eras, so the chapters go.

The house and its residents are well documented in such places as the Norfolk Record Office and Sir John Soane's Museum, and the estate has been included in several surveys and historical accounts. There are many loose ends of course, and no doubt there always will be, but I have tried to list my sources should anyone want to explore further.

It is difficult enough to answer the question 'Why write…?' but the corresponding question needs to be answered: 'Who will read…?'.

Letton Hall is now a house that many people come to visit: not for the reason of the house itself – for a two-hour tour around – and the house is not self-consciously on show, but people come to stay for a weekend or a week or sometimes longer. The present 'life of Letton' is described in the last chapter, so you will arrive at it in due chronological order (unless you are a last-page-first person) but living for even two days here often prompts the question 'What's the story of the house?'. This book is for anyone who feels that question bubbling up.

In searching through the archives of various libraries, museums and record offices, I came across the following quotation. It was on the front cover of *The East Anglian Journal* for the years 1891–2, as a kind of extended motto.

> 'Antiquities are history defaced, or remnants that have escaped the shipwreck of time…wrecks of history wherein the memory of things is almost lost; or such particulars as industrious persons, with exact and scrupulous diligence can any way collect from genealogies, calendars, titles, inscriptions, monuments, coins, names, etymologies, proverbs, traditions, archives, instruments, fragments of private and public history, scattered passages of books no way historical etc., by which means something is recovered from the deluge of time…In this imperfect history, no deficiency need be noted, it being of its own nature, imperfect.
>
> **Francis Bacon** *The Advancement of Learning.*'[1]

It caught my eye. I liked the idea of rescuing something from the deluge of time, remnants that had escaped the shipwreck… and so I present this 'imperfect history'.

---

1   Francis Bacon, *The Advancement of Learning* 1605, Book Two, II (3) and (4).

EARLY LETTON

Any house with even the most modest aspirations to fame has to have a Royal Visit of which to boast. In Letton's case, Queen Elizabeth I ate her sandwiches on the lawns here…

Whenever this claim is put to visitors, there are usually at least one or two will look out respectfully from late Georgian windows onto Victorian lawns, and see it all in their mind's eye. But it is not usually long before the realisation dawns that the dates really don't match up; the present Letton Hall just wasn't there in Elizabeth's time.

However, it isn't all just a figment of imagination or even merely an over- zealous attempt to spice up a guided tour. In Mostyn Armstrong's *History and Antiquities of the County of Norfolk* there is this passage:

> 'Letton, a small village, situated between the two market towns of Dereham and Hingham (written formerly Lacton, as supposed from the richness of its pastures) was famous for its milk and butter; and it is remarked that Queen Elizabeth, while on her progress into Norfolk, and while on her visit at Wood-Rising was supplied with butter three several times from a farm in the town of Letton, so remarkable was it even then for the goodness of its butter.' [1]

It is admittedly a stretch of touristic licence to go from 'partaking of butter' to eating sandwiches on the lawns, particularly as the Earl of Sandwich hadn't by then made his famous invention, but the spirit of the event is there. Certainly two facts are unassailably true: Queen Elizabeth *did* progress into Norfolk and visit Wood-Rising, just a few miles from Letton, and there was a small village of Letton in her time.

However even Mostyn Armstrong may not have had complete faith in his story, for he prefaces it with this note:

> 'We shall now add a short account of this town from a manuscript of authority, and leave our readers to determine how much doctors differ.'

It is not at all certain who the differing doctors are but Mostyn Armstrong mentions earlier a Mr Parkin, who with Rev Francis Blomefield produced *An Essay towards a Topographical History of Norfolk* [2] – which just might be the 'the manuscript of authority'. This is mere speculation (especially in the light of publication dates), but it all seems to make a good story with which to start a history of Letton Hall.

Another aspect on which 'doctors *do* differ' is the derivation of the name Letton. Mostyn Armstrong's source claims it is from *Lacton*, and therefore to do with milk (from the Latin 'lactus'). On the other hand, the *Dictionary of English Place Names* [3] thinks that *Lecton* is from the Old English *Lece* meaning 'brook'. In the Historical Atlas of Norfolk [4] '-tun' refers to a farm or settlement i.e. a smaller place than a '– ham' which is a village or estate. To add to the confusion, there are three mentions of Letton, or Letton variants in Domesday: *Letetuna*, *Lettuna* and *Letuna*.

1:1 Aerial photograph of Letton taken by the RAF in 1946. The ruins of All Saints Church can be seen at the bottom right of the picture, together with the tracks and house platforms of the old village of Letton. An interpretive map of this photograph is included in Appendix I.

THE VILLAGE AND CHURCH OF LETTON

Whatever the uncertainties over the derivations of the name, the village of Letton certainly existed, although it can now be said to have disappeared almost completely. The one possible surviving building, much altered over the years, is the lodge at the Cranworth end of the driveway.

The aerial view of Letton (**1:1**), taken by the RAF in 1946, clearly shows evidence of the village, to the right of the present-day semi-circular driveway. There is a trace still visible over the parkland today of the 'hollow way' running from the ruins of the church (in the copse at the bottom right of the picture) down to the small pond to the left of it. A full interpretive map of this photograph is included with other maps as Appendix I.

Some comprehensive research has been carried out on Letton and a number of other similar villages by Alan Davison and has been published by the Norfolk Archaeological Unit of the Norfolk Museums Service [5]. It is outside the scope of this present book to go into great detail on the village itself, but the account of events leading up to the building of the hall is interesting.

There is evidence of sheep farming and weaving, with a metal-worker dwelling there, and also of a water-mill on the small headwater of the Blackwater river. There may also have been a brick kiln in the 18th century, but the village was not near any turnpike roads or great estates and was off the beaten track.

It was never very large, up to a maximum of 100 inhabitants, but it did boast the church of All Saints until this fell into ruin; after which the village became a spread-out community of yeoman farmers dominated by the mansion house. Quoting from the book's summary:

> 'The village seems to have been somewhat poorer than its immediate neighbours, and of moderate importance only in the Hundred of Mitford. Its demise appears to have been gradual and can be attributed to no obvious cause, though there are indications that the presence of manorial sheep flocks may have contributed in late medieval and early post-medieval times. By the seventeenth century the settlement had became a community of scattered farms, many of which were on the margins of the Green. Some further shrinkage in the eighteenth century seems to have made easier the disappearance of Letton Green, and the building between 1785 and 1788 of Letton Hall, replacing an older mansion house, in a much enlarged park.' [6]

The moving of some of the nearby roads, as described in the Road Order Maps in Appendix I, also had an effect on the decline of the village. The church is of interest too, with indications that it may have been quite ornate and elaborately furnished. George and Alayne Fenner say this about it.

> 'The Church of All Saints in Domesday Book and the Advowson was given to Lewes Priory in the twelfth century by Gilbert de Rysing. It was consolidated with Cranworth in 1546, was ruinous by 1560 and today has virtually disappeared.
>
> Information from wills of the fifteenth and early sixteenth century suggest that the church consisted of nave, chancel and north aisle with a holy water stoup at the north door, side altars, and Easter Sepulchre and a 'Glasse Wyndow at our Lady's Awter'.
>
> Investigation of the undergrowth of the heavily wooded site revealed some traces of flint foundations, which indicates a church of two aisles and a chancel. There was a thick cover of nettles and Dogs-mercury over the presumed graveyard area.
>
> Some fourteen metres from the west end of the church was a flint feature around three metres in diameter, but it was impossible to tell if this was the foundations of a tower or just a heap of demolition rubble. Wood-Rising Hall (now demolished) is reputed to having contained stone from Letton Church.

A Gothic summerhouse in the gardens of Letton Hall also contains much medieval carved stone, and three Perpendicular-style three-light windows, which may have come from the church. However, the tracery of two of these is similar to that in the chancel windows of neighbouring Shipdham church which underwent a thorough Victorian renewal. The owner of Letton Hall was proprietor of Shipdham church at that time'.[7]

Mostyn Armstrong adds confirmation on the fate of the church.

'The church of Letton which was dedicated to All Saints, was pulled down in 1535 by Sir Richard Southwell, and the materials theeof carried to rebuild Rising Hall which in 17?? was entirely pulled down, leaving only the farmhouse.' [8]

Another reference to this is contained in the Colman Collection in the Norfolk Record Office. A 17th-century copy of the Union in 1546 of the Parishes of Letton and Cranworth states: 'Letton was ye church demolished by R(obert) S(outhwell) to build an appartement belonging to the house at Wood Rising'.[9]

THE ORIGINAL LETTON HALL

Only one picture seems to exist of the original Letton Hall (**1:2**). Its location has not been established for certain but it is likely that it was about 200 yards north of the present hall. There is a boomerang-shaped lake there now (see the interpretive map in Appendix I) with sides of brickwork that could well be house foundations. In her *History of Letton Park* Anthea Taigel makes some interesting observations on the picture.

LETTON HALL.

The Seat of Thornhagh Gurdon, Esq.ᵣ

Publish'd as the Act directs, June 4ᵗʰ1781, by M.Booth, Norwich.

1:2 The only known picture of the original Letton Hall, published in 1781.

'This shows a rather curious building which is obviously of more than one period. It had ten bays with a three-storied porch and central cupola with ball finial.

A large walled forecourt in front of the house extended the full width of the façade. The front wall of the court was low, about half the height of the other two walls. It appears strangely out of scale with the very high gate piers, which flagged a single iron gateway in the centre of the wall, and may have been lowered from its' original height (or it may have been the exercise of 'artistic license' in the illustration to allow for a view of the house over this wall).' [10]

One can imagine from the picture how this house just 'grew' wing by wing; over the years as lands and wealth were added to the estate, so more rooms were needed. However, the individual rooms would have remained small in keeping with the scale of the original house, so the layout would not have been appropriate for a grander lifestyle.

The Brampton family had held land in Letton for many generations but when Amye Brampton married John Gurdon of Assington in Suffolk the stage was set for major advances in the estate. The Brampton Gurdon family were still living in the old hall in the 1780s but it was then to be replaced by a new Letton Hall built by John Soane.

1   Mostyn Armstrong, editor, *History and Antiquities in the County of Norfolk*, 1781, volume 8, p44.

2   F Blomefield, *An Essay Towards a Topographical History of the County of Norfolk*, 1805–10.

3   E Ekwall, editor, *Dictionary of English Place Names*, 1960.

4   *An Historical Atlas of Norfolk*, published by the Norfolk Museums Service and others, 1993. An article by Dr Tom Williamson on place-name patterns appears on page 44.

5   Alan Davison, *Six Deserted Villages of Norfolk*, East Anglian Archaeology EAA44, published by the Norfolk Archaeology Unit, 1988.

6   Ibid, p38.

7   Ibid, pages 46-7.

8   See ref (1) above, p45.

9   Norfolk Record Office, Colman MSS, CO/13/51,2.

10 Anthea Taigel, *A History of Letton Park*, Centre of East Anglian Studies UEA 1990, unpublished.

DILLINGHAM BRAMPTON GURDON DILLINGHAM

There was a lot at stake when in 1740 the next heir to the Letton lands was born. Fortunes could be lost. His father's three brothers had died young, and he himself was an only child; and, apart from him, there was no male heir to the substantial wealth on his mother's side either.

According to family tradition he was named Brampton Gurdon but this time there were other factors to be taken into account. His mother, Sarah, was the daughter of Theophilus Dillingham of Bedfordshire and since her only brother had died young there was no male heir to inherit the Dillingham fortune. So it was that when her own son was born he was named Dillingham Brampton Gurdon. However, when Theophilus Dillingham died in 1768, under the terms of the will Dillingham Brampton Gurdon became Brampton Gurdon Dillingham.

Whatever the inconveniences of having a complicated and changing name, and whatever the confusion it causes historical researchers, the arrangement achieved the desired effect: he inherited the fortune.

It seems probable that the old Letton Hall was quite full of family members when he was a child. Although his Gurdon grandfather had died a few years before he was born, his grandmother lived until the young Dillingham Brampton Gurdon was five. Sadly his mother died when he was only 14, but his father had two elder sisters, Jane and Elizabeth, who kept house. Jane died when Dillingham Brampton Gurdon was 20 years old, but by then he had launched out on his own life. His Aunt Elizabeth however remained a key figure in his life for many years.

In the light of the heavy responsibility riding on the shoulders of the young Dillingham Brampton Gurdon it is easy to imagine him being cosseted and pampered and fussed over. The picture of him (**2:1**) in what appears to be a young girl's dress could give that impression, but it is more an indication of the custom and fashion of the times than anything else. Certainly, whatever attentions he received didn't stop Dillingham Brampton Gurdon living a full and active life. (**2:2**).

He was awarded a Bachelor of Arts degree from Clare Hall, Cambridge in 1762 when he was 22 years old, and must have been well regarded while there for he was offered an Honorary Fellowship in March 1763. In 1765 he received his MA degree. But a major preoccupation during his early twenties was his courtship of Miss Maria Bedingfield.

THE LOVE STORY

Maria Bedingfield (**2:3**) was the daughter of Mr Philip Bedingfield of Ditchingham, with links with the Bedingfields of Oxburgh Hall, Norfolk dating back to the 14th century [1].

2:1 A portrait of Dillingham Brampton Gurdon as a young boy.
PORTRAIT REPRODUCED BY COURTESY OF LORD CRANWORTH

Dillingham Brampton Gurdon courts her with such assiduity and floweriness of language and obvious adoration that we begin to see her for ourselves on the pedestal on which he places her.

In the private Gurdon papers [2], there are several letters addressed to Miss Maria Bedingfield which allow us a fascinating inside view of this charming love story. It has its difficult times 'for the course of true love never did run smooth', but their happiness shines through. Dillingham Brampton Gurdon's handwriting is very difficult to decipher in places, and sometimes the ink and paper he used hasn't lasted well; some of the transcripts are therefore not complete, but there is plenty to go on. In order to give as full an idea of the correspondence as possible, a few letters are quoted completely, with extracts from others.

2:2 Brampton Gurdon Dillingham (1740–1820) at the age of 45, painted by Walton.
PORTRAIT REPRODUCED BY COURTESY OF LORD CRANWORTH

The letters are written and addressed in the usual way for the time. The paper is folded three or more commonly four times, so that no text is visible from the outside, then sealed with wax and the address written on the outside of the letter itself, without using an envelope. The delivery instructions, and the addresses Maria is asked to use, demanded a great deal of resourcefulness from the postal system. For example:

> 'To Miss Bedingfield at Ditchingham. To be left at the Red Lyon in St. Stephen's for the Bungay Carrier.'

> 'I desire you to direct to me at Theophilus Dillingham's at Hampton near the Court, Middlesex' 13th February 1762

2:3 Maria Dillingham Gurdon (née Bedingfield) 1741–69.
PORTRAIT REPRODUCED BY COURTESY OF LORD CRANWORTH)

'Pray direct to me at Mr Sterck's, Watchmaker, Portugal Street, Lincoln's Inn, London'
15th March 1763

'I hope this will reach you without fail by the Coach…' 14th August 1763

Several themes recur throughout the letters; one is the difficulty of travel. Considering the time of year at which he is writing this first letter, and the 'road' conditions that existed and the journeys he seemed to be so often undertaking, Dillingham Brampton Gurdon seems to make surprisingly little of it.

He obviously hates leaving Maria and in this letter and in many others he entreats her to write regularly. Amidst all this, there are little touches of love and the 'exchanges of tokens'. In this letter it is something that dropped out of her watch. A note? A small picture? A lock of hair?...We aren't to know, but similar details occur in other letters also.

Finally in this letter, he touches on the vital topic of *Parental Permission to Marry*.

'Letton
13th February 1762

I have the satisfaction of being able to inform you, my Dearest, of my arrival here between one and two yesterday, without being carried away by the Inundation of Waters which I was forced to pass at two Places; I hope you went home yesterday afternoon, for you must have had a dismal journey if you stayed till this morning; bad as our prospect is, we are to set forward tomorrow morning thro' all the snow for London.

I was so wholly immersed in the unhappy thought of parting from you for so unsupportable a length of time, that I entirely forgot to deliver to you something which you dropped from your watch at my Aunt's, and which I have sent enclosed, and hope it will come safe to you.

As yesterday separated me from your presence, and almost overcame me by the melancholy length of that dismal prospect before me of two months' long <u>long</u> separation from the only object of my Happiness, so tomorrow will carry me out of Norfolk, most dear to me, as it contains my only pledge of Happiness, my Life, my <u>all</u>; but be assured, my Dearest, my Heart, my Thoughts, will be ever here – and that distance of Time or Place can never have any effect on Hearts so nearly, so strongly connected, as yours and mine are.

As it will be impossible to support this tedious separation without a frequent and punctual correspondence, I must entreat you to give me that satisfaction as frequently as you possibly can. I assure you it shall never rest long on my side. If you are so kind as to make use of Saturday's Post, I shall be so happy as to receive it on the Tuesday.

I long much for that time not only on that account, but also because I am very impatient to have the first interview and discussion of our Affairs over between the old Gentlemen. My Father desires me to remember his particular Compts. to you, and all the Family. Adieu, my Love, receive the warmest wishes for your welfare of your most devoted

D.B. Gurdon.' **3**

At the time of the next letter included here Dillingham Brampton Gurdon has been away for three months; part of the time in Hampton with his grandfather Theophilus Dillingham, and at least some of the rest of the time in Essex. He has obviously missed Maria a great deal. In this 'five minute note' there is less emphasis on keeping up the correspondence, because he is going to visit her in five days time. 'Present my best respects to Mr and Mrs Bedingfield and family, inform them of my Design of Paying Respects to them' has a modern day translation of 'tell your parents I'm inviting myself to stay...'.

'Letton, Sunday morn. [1762, exact date uncertain]

I fear my Dearest Maria has begun for several Days to accuse me of inexcusable neglect and carelessness, in not giving her any further account of my motions for this fortnight past. But believe me, my Dearest, I could not think of any way of sending a letter out of Essex so as to reach Ditchingham sooner than if I stayed till I reached Norfolk. I arrived here only yesterday. The Thanksgiving Day kept us two days longer in Essex than was at first designed.

During my stay there I first took a Trip for one day to see your Brother at Cambridge. I had the satisfaction of hearing by my friend Partridge last night that you were all well a few days since; as he returns to Norwich this evening, I hope you'll excuse the shortness of this Epistle, for I have not above five minutes left, which I shall most joyfully seize to inform you of my Design of repairing to the true Country Retirement, as you are pleased to term it, at Ditchingham on Friday morning next. And in Sir Ant. Branville's Phrase, of then prostrating myself at your Feet, and surrendering myself at Discretion into your Prison, which I have so impatiently longed for these last three Months.

I have looked upon all that Liberty, and fashionable round of Diversions in Town, which you think has detained me there so long, as nothing better than a long intolerable course of Banishment from the one Place where I have ever found, or can ever hope to find, solid Happiness.

The Time obliges me to conclude this scrawl, only begging you to present my best Respects to Mr and Mrs Bedingfield and Family and to inform them of my Design of paying my Respects to them next Friday.

Whilst for these five tedious days, suspense is on the wing, I support myself with the Enjoyment of Ideal Pleasure, and by anticipating those real Joys which I hope for at our Happy Meeting.

Adieu till then, my Dearest. Believe me to be, with the most unfeigned Affection, Most devotedly yours

D.B. Gurdon.

My Father desires his particular Compliments to yourself and Family. I fear you cannot read this vile scrawl.'[4]

Despite being only twenty-two, with Maria only twenty-one, and despite hearing some of his elders 'expatiating on ye ill effects of early marriages', Dillingham Brampton Gurdon is determined to press on with his plans for marriage. He writes from Letton on the 29th May 1762.

'The point I Yesterday evening moved to my Father, and am overjoyed at the Happiness of being able to inform you …I have obtained his Leave for the accomplishing our happy union so as for us to fix at Michaelmass. For which purpose my Father will meet Mr B [her father] very soon, when I hope every Thing will be settled to the satisfaction of all Parties.

This happy Approach of the End of our long Prospect fills me with Joy, that I cannot attempt to express. For then, my Love, these Pains of Absence and Parting will be no more, but will I hope, with God's Blessing, be succeeded by an uninterrupted course of happy union and Enjoyment of each other.'[5]

Throughout the correspondence both families seem to be content with the way things are progressing, visiting each other from time to time and 'desiring Particular compliments' to be exchanged by the letters. The couple are now well on their way to receiving full parental support but there is still one major obstacle; the formal consent of Grandfather Theophilus Dillingham, and with it, the full financial support needed before Dillingham Brampton Gurdon comes into his eventual inheritance.

The circumstances behind the next letter are that Dillingham Brampton Gurdon has sent a trusted friend to plead his case with his grandfather, expecting the answer 'yes'. To his dismay, Theophilus Dillingham expresses reluctance to give his outright consent and, more importantly, doesn't offer any help other than occasional financial support. Dillingham Brampton Gurdon immediately dashes off this letter to his prospective father-in-law, in something approaching dismay.

To Philip Bedingfield from Clare Hall [Cambridge]   Novr 25th [1762]
Dear Sir

At the time when I hoped to have been able to have given you an account of having successfully concluded our negotiations, I am less able to bear up against the bad news which I yesterday received from my friend, who has been to my grandfather, at my request directly to ask his consent that it might go forward.

The old gentleman upon hearing directly Miss B's fortune has expatiated very much upon ye imprudence of it, and that he will have no concern in it one way or other; but that my father and I may act in it as we think proper without any dependence on him. My friend assures me that he cannot give me encouragement to expect any certain present assistance from him, but only occasional presents by way of immediate assistance, as he may think proper.

This is a cruel stroke and reduces me, as to certainty, to that assistance alone which my father, as I informed you, has promised to give me, and which you know is very slender.

I was less prepared to support this unexpected ill-fortune, because when this gentleman sounded him before upon it…he expressed not ye least dislike, but merely that he should not meddle in our affairs and hinted as I informed you…he could not mention directly of fortune but only in general that there was a large family, and therefore that it could not be expected to be large.

You see ye great difficulties this cruel resolution has laid me under. I shall write to my father for his sente-mento on the occasion, but I am going first tomorrow to my friend in London to consult with him what steps I shall take with ye old gentleman to remove if possible his unkind resolution…

I shall stay very few days in town, and shall esteem it as a particular favour if you would be so kind as to give me your sentiments on the occasion. I beg my best respects to Mrs Bedingfield and Mrs Bacon. Nor can I conclude this without expressing in the strongest terms ye sense I have of great civilities here, and have repeatably received from yourself and Mrs Bedingfield; I am sir

your most obliged and most obedient servant

Dill. B. Gurdon.' [6]

But all turns out not as black as it appears. By the time of this next letter Dillingham Brampton Gurdon has had a week in which to work on the situation, and to consider the options. He has been to visit his grandfather personally, and has been well received. He writes to Maria in an entirely different frame of mind. The crisis is over.

'London   Decr. 2 [1762]

Dearest Life,

I have the happiness of being able to inform you that the thick cloud which seemed to hang so heavily over me last week is dispersed. When I troubled you with a gloomy account I was so dispirited that I feared things worse than I found them – I have been with ye old gentleman, and was received very affectionately and in great good humour, and tho he declared that if he had known of ye affair sometime since, he must have endeavoured to have dissuaded me upon that consideration which I from my soul despise. Yet as things are, he shall not concern himself by interfering one way or other.

…He will make no bargain, but shall occasionally assist me from time to time by way of addition to my income, and will not suffer me to be in want of money, which are his own words. Thus my Dearest, ye storm is happily dispersed. When I feared his displeasure I was received with the greatest kindness, and had from his own mouth an assurance of being assisted from time to time, which is all I could desire. ……

I hope this account will be satisfactory to you and Mrs Bedingfield. I assure you it is quite so to me, for I know his generosity so well, tho he will not part with the staff out of his hands, as he says I cannot claim it, yet he will never suffer me to be in any difficulties for want of his assistance.

I hope now there is no further room for any obstacle to my happiness, which I now flatter myself will soon be absolutely fixed. I return to Cambridge tomorrow, and hope to be in Norfolk about Christmas. I wait most impatiently for our next happy meeting, when I hope everything will be fixed immovably.

I am now very sorry that I communicated to you the gloomy account of last week, which must have been very disagreeable; I hope this will entirely disperse any ill-effect of it; for anything that gives of least uneasiness to you, must, you are very sensible, give me the greatest pain.

Your most Devoted

BDG

Please excuse the trim of my pen and paper for I could get no better.' [7]

There is now a gap of a few months in the correspondence. Once the paramount matter of permission to marry is settled, other areas of life can continue. In this next letter it is brought home that although in one respect we are merely following the course of a story that could be that of any couple in love, in another we are seeing something of the privileged life of an able and rich young man.

And we also learn that his grandfather is being as generous as he promised!

'From Hampton   Mar15 [1763]

You were excessively kind, my Dearest Maria, in so soon indulging your humble slave with your last favour. The length of time which it has been suffered to lay unanswered may justly appear to you to be inexcusable, but the circumstances of the case, will, I hope, plead its own excuses. I must then acquaint you that I have taken a very sudden and unexpected trip to Cambridge upon an Invitation from the Master and Fellows of Clare Hall to accept of an Honorary Fellowship in Testimony of their approbation of my conduct; I at first doubted whether in the situation I am now so happy as to be, it was worthwhile, but as it was offered in so polite a manner and seemed to give great satisfaction to both the old gentlemen, I determined to go down and accept it.

As I left this place last Thursday night, your kind favour just missed me, and I had not the happiness of receiving it till I returned hither last Friday. During my absence from hence I spent three days in Town, and absolutely at my own power, I made the best use of my time.

Thursday evening I saw Mr Sheridan's new comedy; it is acted inimitably well, and I am so very unfashionable as to be much pleased with it. It is too moral and sentimental to please the depravity of most minds, and as such it has [many] violently against it, as dull and tedious. For my part I must own I have not met with a theatrical performance for a great while, that has given me so much satisfaction. Most of the characters seem to be drawn very natural, and possibly a sympathy with some of the sentiments made it have a stronger effect upon me. Frequent interspersions of the truly high-wrought ridiculous character of Sir Anthony cannot fail to furnish occasion of mirth. I am very glad to find you agree with me in liking it. I hope it precedes in some measure from a sympathy in those sentimentals before mentioned…

I find I have undesignedly been led upon this subject to fill up the greatest part of the paper. I must proceed to tell you that I intended on Friday event, to have been at Dr Browns's new oratorio but was prevented. Saturday I was at the opera, a diversion which did not give me much entertainment. But some of the airs in the opera of Ivione are so fine, and the principal female voice there this season so angelic, that I don't know when I have been in higher musical raptures. Could I but have had you with me, I had called myself happy.

Tomorrow we leave this place and go to stay in Town where I shall hope to be soon favoured with a few lines from you. I must entreat you not to retaliate upon my long silence, which you see could not be avoided.

I am very happy in being able to inform you that my old gentleman here has been very kind to me, and has shown the sincerity of his intentions in what he before declared.

I beg my Particular Respects to all friends with you, and most affect. remembrances to your brother whom I shall be glad to hear from. Believe me, my dearest to be the greatest warmth and sincerity of affection,

yours

Dill. B. Gurdon' [8]

The wedding is fixed. The money is fixed. All that remains are some of those inescapable details of the ceremony and of the setting up of home that all couples have to deal with…

'14th August 1763

Amidst the multiplicity of anxious thoughts that crowded into my mind before I left Ditchingham, it entirely escaped my mind to take the size of your little finger for a diamond ring. I beg you'll be so kind as to contrive to give it to me in your next, without which I don't know how my neglect can be rectified.' [9]

'Saturday noon [1763, exact date unknown]

I am very happy, my Dearest, in being able to acquaint you that your epistle had the desired effect; my father desires his compts to you, and says as you are very desirous of it, he is very willing to oblige you in that or anything else. …He readily consents to our putting up crimson paper in the parlour, if you comply with the other scheme proposed. I also found here a ticker for the hall, which my father had procured for me of Hindmarsh. I am going up to thank him for it, so I must entreat meeting you there if any possible means be, should things fall out unluckily. I beg respects and compts to all. I am most devotedly,

Yours,

D.B. Gurdon'[10]

In looking forward to their marriage a few weeks away he allows himself just one more regret about being apart:

'…before that union, the object of my long and constant wishes, will take place – which I pray may be attended with that constant and uninterrupted happiness which our most ardent wishes can desire. I trust, my Dearest, this will be the case with God's blessing….'[11]

They were married in the late summer of 1763, and the courtship correspondence between them comes to an end.

FAMILY LIFE

By all accounts the Gurdons were very happy after their marriage and were no doubt thrilled when their first son was born a year or so afterwards. Breaking with the family tradition and perhaps mindful of from where their means came, they named him Theophilus Thornhagh, after his grandfather and great-grandfather. Thornhagh Philip arrived the following year in

1765, and Philip Brampton was to be born two years later in 1767.

They lived in Norwich at this time, probably in the house the family had in the Cathedral Close, and were still, being in their early 20s, a young couple. From 1776 however, after only three years of marriage and at only 25 years old, Mrs Gurdon (now calling herself Mary in her letters) ominously began to feel unwell.

During her pregnancy with Philip, she wrote an interesting letter that gives a detailed picture of the family's life at the time. She had left Norwich to spend a short time at her parents house at Ditchingham, in 'her present circumstances' (i.e. pregnant), when she hears to her dismay that her younger son Thornhagh, then aged about two, has picked up whooping cough. The two boys had been left at Norwich in the charge of her aunt, Miss Elizabeth Gurdon and their doctor Mr Donnes, who jointly wrote telling her about the illness. Mary Gurdon is most alarmed, and wants Thornhagh to be taken straight off to Letton for a change of air. She is unable to do this herself, so asks if her aunt will arrange it all. Other people mentioned in the letter include Mrs Firs, the housekeeper at Letton, the children's nurse, and Mary and Johnson, servants at the Norwich house. Theophilus, aged three at this time, is to remain in Norwich until his mother can return in a week or so.

'**Mrs Mary Gurdon to Miss Elizabeth Gurdon**   15 May 1767

Dear Madam

I am much concerned to find by your and Mr Donnes letter, that my poor little Thornhagh has picked up the whooping cough; a dreadful complaint at any time, but more particularly so to him, as he has still his teeth to struggle with; but I hope God as he has it but in a slight degree that he will not labour long under it.

I am very desirous he should have a change of air as soon as possible; as I am convinced it is the only that can be of use in that disorder. I would therefore have Nurse, with Mr Donnes consent, go with him to Letton as soon next week as you think the nursery and bed can be properly air'd for him. I am firmly of the opinion that if he has an immediate change of air it will prevent the cough from getting ahead of him. I am quite ashamed to give you so much trouble as to write to Mrs Firs to inform her of the childs going there; but shall esteem it a particular favour if you will give her a line tomorrow to request her to air the bed and room extremely well, and likewise tell her what day you shall send the child and Nurse.

I have wrote to Bath to acquaint my Father with the liberty I intend taking and flatter myself in such an exivence, he will pardon my doing it without his leave, as to have waited for his concurrence, which I could not have under ten days, would have given the cough much too long a time to have got ahead of the child, and have made it much more difficult to conquer.

All my friends here persuaded me to have no time lost in trying what change of air will do, which they found of infinite benefit to Francis under the same complaint last summer. They are more particularly solicitous that I should send him into the country as they think it very unsafe for me to venture home to him, and indeed under my present circumstances, I should be very apprehensive for myself as I know not if I should catch it but it might prove fatal to me.

I intend returning to Norwich the latter end of next week or the beginning of the week following if I can persuade my Father to part with me, and desire till I return that Mary and Johnson would be particularly careful and attentive to my dear Theophilus, who I am rejoiced to hear is so well.

I beg you would be so good as to give Nurse directions to take everything with her she thinks can possibly be wanting; some prunes and senna to stew, some manna or any other cooling physic Mr Donne shall order Thornhagh to take, some watch candle, biscuits and sugar lest Mrs Firs should not have a supply of those things, and likewise to be sure to let you know always by the carrier how the child is. I desire she would have a light bread or batter pudding made for him every day and be particularly careful not to let him eat dumplings, beef or pork when he gets to Letton; for it is very necessary that his stomach should be kept in good order, and he should eat nothing but what is light of digestion.

I am quite ashamed at the trouble I am giving you, and would have come over and given these orders myself, but as I have no carriage here I did not know how to do it comfortably.

I would by no means have John return the same day from Letton, but stay and come back the next morning that the horses may have time to rest.

I would beg favour of you to direct Nurse in whatever you think proper and to purchase anything you think the child may want, did I not fear you would think me most impertinently troublesome; but as I am at present circumstanc'd I flatter myself you will, my dear Madam, be so kind to excuse the liberties I have taken; I can assure you it is with greatest reluctance I have given you all this trouble.

I hope you continue well and shall be glad to hear from you about the middle of next week, if you have a few minutes to spare.

All this family desire to join in all our compts, dear Madam

Your affect. niece

M.Gurdon

A kiss for my dear babes.

I have wrote this letter so ill that I am afraid you will hardly be able to make it out but I have very bad materials and write rather in a hurry, so hope you will excuse it.' [12]

Thornhagh recovers completely from his illness, and goes on to live a healthy life for many years to come. Theophilus, too, seems to suffer no problems, and later in 1767 Philip Brampton is born safely.

But the illness with which Mary was beginning to suffer gets worse. By the summer of 1768, she is unable to fulfil her role in the family and goes to 'take the air' at Great Yarmouth. The following letter (**2:4**) shows with what courage she tackled her cure, and what desire and determination she had to return to 'attend to my dear little boys'. 'I long to see them' she says.

'Mrs Mary Gurdon to Miss Elizabeth Gurdon   Yarmouth, 29 September 1768

Dear Madam

I have long promised myself the pleasure of addressing you, but have ever been prevented by one avocation or other, for what with riding and things etc, my time has been much engrossed; I know it will give you pleasure that I can boast of being amazingly the better for my expedition to this place, and think I may now, I thank God, affirm that I am well as I have been these two years. The bathing agrees so much with me that I am almost insensible to cold the whole day after it, and can bear the cold east winds from the sea to blow upon me without so much as shivering.

I now flatter myself that I shall again, with God's blessing, recover such a state of health as to be able to attend to my dear little boys, and with the assistance of their good Father to cultivate those tender and dear pledges to our mutual happiness; I hope they are tractable and good boys, and that they are not troublesome to you and my father. I am sure we are much indebted to both him and you for your kind care of them, I hope my dear Theophilus does not forget his humour and other little things that I had taken pains to teach him. My dear Thornhagh has nothing to lose and is not much indebted at present to me for instruction but I hope we shall do better ere it be long. Pray remember me affectionately to them both, I long to see them.

I was much pleased to hear by my good man that you were not much suffered by the attack upon your Hotel, and congratulate you upon your escape. I doubt it will fill my cousin with apprehensions the whole winter, for her timid disposition will paint a thousand dangers in her imagination. I hope my father has lost his cold. I am sorry he would not come and take a dip with me in the sea as I think it would be of use to him, and fortify him against those perpetual colds which he is so subject to. The weather is now delightful and the water by no means cold.

There is no news stirring in this place so that I fear you will be tired with reading so dull an epistle, I will therefore release you, only adding the compts and respects of all my small family to my father and yourself, not excepting our love to our dear boys and beg you will believe that I am with the sincerest respect,

Your affectionate niece and obliged servant

M. Gurdon'[13]

Her optimism about returning to full health was not well founded however. From other references in the letters (for instance, about one of the boys 'with a cough vastly like his mothers') it is clear that she was suffering from 'consumption' i.e. pulmonary tuberculosis, and in reality, no amount of sea air or bathing was likely to cure her.

2:4 A facsimile of Mary Gordon's letter to her aunt, written on 29 September 1768. This page includes the first two paragraphs of the letter plus, on the left hand side, the address and seal. The folds, which enable the contents to be concealed leaving only the address visible until the seal is broken, can just be seen.

REPRODUCED BY COURTESY OF LORD CRANWORTH

TRAGEDY

Having struggled courageously but in vain with her illness Mary Gurdon died on 27 June 1769 aged 28 and is buried in St Mary's church, Cranworth. The inscription on the ledger stone reads:

> Underneath this stone lie
> the remains of Mary
> the much beloved wife of
> Brampton Gurdon Dillingham
> Who quitted this vale of misery
> for a happy immortality.

From such happy beginnings, her life must have seemed truly a vale of misery in those last years. She may have been given release from it, but her husband and sons went on grieving.

As well as the inscription on the floor of the church, there is also a memorial tablet on the wall, beautifully carved from white marble (**2:5**). Often such church memorials are remote and impersonal, but this one is alive with the emotions of a young family grieving for wife and mother. The boys were aged five, four and two.

> Sacred to the memory of MARY
> The much beloved Wife of
> Brampton Gurdon Dillingham Esq.
> And Daughter of Philip Bedingfield Esq.
> of Ditchingham
> By Mary his first Wife
> Daughter of Sr. Edmund Bacon of Gillingham Bart.
>
> A most excellent Woman
> A sincere and devout Christian
> Virtuous Discreet Good
> An exemplary Pattern
> Of Christian Meekness, Patience and Resignation
> A Shining Example of Filial Duty
> Conjugal Affection and Parental Care and Tenderness
>
> To perpetuate such eminent Virtues
> Her sorrowful Husband
> Has caused them to be engraved
> On this Monument of Marble
> Already engraved more deeply
> On his own Heart
>
> She died the 27th day of June 1769
> After a long and lingering Illness
> Which carried her off
> In the 28th year of her Age
>
> And left behind her three infant sons
> Theophilus Thornhagh, Thornhagh Philip
> and Philip Brampton
> To bewail with their afflicted father
> Their inestimable loss.

2:5 The memorial to Mary Gurdon, on the wall of St Mary's Church, Cranworth

There is just one more letter we have from Brampton Gurdon Dillingham, this one to his old family friend William Brocket. Notice he is now 'B.G. Dillingham' not 'D.B. Gurdon'. Old Theophilus Dillingham had died in 1768, so the Dillingham surname had been passed on. Strictly speaking, Mary had died 'Mrs Dillingham', not 'Mrs Gurdon', but this was of little consequence in the tragic and poignant circumstances.

'Brampton Gurdon Dillingham to William Brocket   Norwich July 13 1769

My Dear Sir

I need not express to you who have been a partner in the like affliction the state of misery to which the late heavy stroke has reduced me, fallen at once from such a perfect happiness as few ever obtain, to a condition that is both void of present comfort and further prospect; my views of life are all at an end, tho' so early in my life, and I have nothing now left to attach me in this world, save these poor pledges of our faithful love, my helpless babes, now left to my feeble care to rear and guide through this vale of sorrow.

I intended to have moved next Monday towards Hampton with my poor children for three weeks or a month, where my unavoidable business for some hours in the day must have engrossed my thoughts, but I find I cannot get off going to Letton for next week. I shall stop two or three days at Assington the week after, and purpose being at Hampton on the 29 inst. Saturday, which I take to be just the time of your going to fetch Billy. If it is, I hope you'll be so kind to let me find you there, and stop a few days with me; of which I will beg the favour of your answer by a letter to Letton as soon as you receive this.

After that my brother P.B. will stay there with me.

With compts. to all from our house,

I am yours most affectionately
B. Gurdon Dillingham' [14]

The tone of this letter is of a broken man struggling to cope with grief by immersing himself in the minutiae of every-day duties.

From this point we know very little about the life of Brampton Gurdon Dillingham for nearly ten years. He was 29 years old when his wife died, and when we next hear of him he is 39, and his three sons are teenagers. Did he go back to live at Letton with his father and his aunt, where there would be some family life? Or did he remain at the Norwich house where he and Mary had made such a happy home? Or were those memories too difficult to bear?

Was it a question of not wanting to forget, but not being able to bear remembering? He had courted his wife with such intense passion, that perhaps now he had to withdraw from life for a while with his motherless sons, and grieve with the same intensity.

NEW FAMILY DEVELOPMENTS

In 1779 Elizabeth Gurdon died at the age of 83, a little over ten years after the death of her niece. A year or so after that Brampton Gurdon Dillingham married for the second time, to another Mary.

Mary Howard was the daughter of Samuel Howard Esq of Brockdish in Norfolk, and was nine years younger than her husband. She was 30 years old at the time of her marriage, and she and her husband were to have a marriage lasting for 40 years; and for Letton they were going to be very eventful years.

Mary's sister Elizabeth, with whom she was co-heiress, was the wife of the Reverend Peter Forster. The family name of Forster appears in earlier correspondence, which may provide a clue as to how introductions were first made and how the marriage came about.

FAMILY TREE OF THE GURDONS, WHILST AT LETTON HALL

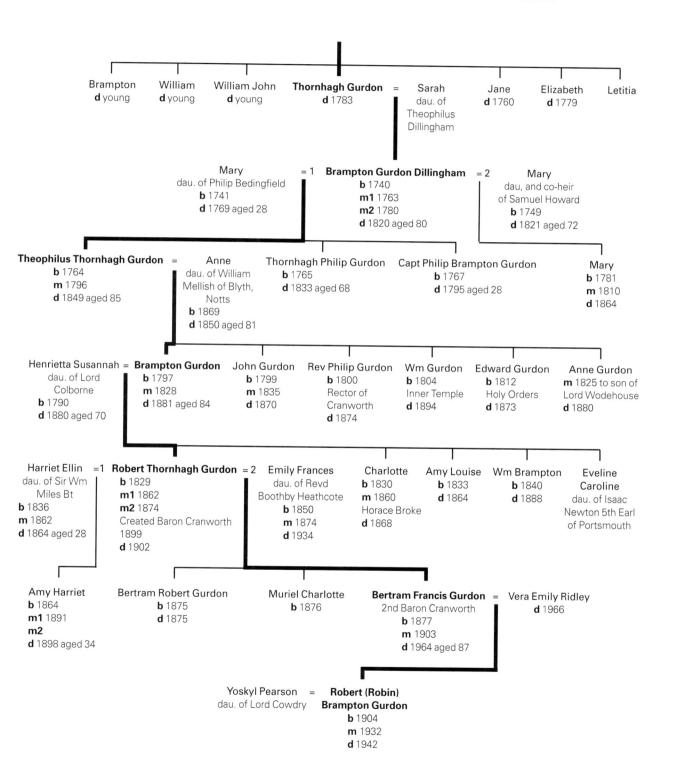

In 1781, Mr and Mrs Brampton Gurdon Dillingham had a daughter, and she became the third Mary in the family, as if to emphasise the fact that life had now moved onwards from the tragedy of the first Mary's death. Certainly family life was going to be different from now on, with a baby girl joining her three brothers aged 14, 16 and 17.

One more event was to shape the new life of Brampton Gurdon Dillingham. His father, Thornhagh, who had lived through so much tragedy and change, himself died in February 1783 at the age of 83. The new heir took over the estate, aged 43 and entered a new era of his life which would involve more change than even he had already lived through; changes that started as John Soane, an up-and-coming young architect, rode over to Letton from Norwich.

1 William Playfair, *British Family Antiquity,* 1811, p518 ff.

2 The private documents and correspondence of the Gurdon family (the Gurdon Papers) are held by Lord Cranworth, as head of the family. Access to these was generously provided for the author, who now holds transcripts of the relevant documents on file.

3 Gurdon Papers Vol. XI p18.

4 Ibid. Vol. XI p18.

5 Ibid. Vol. XI p18.

6 Ibid. Vol. IV p14.

7 Ibid. Vol. IV p16.

8 Ibid. Vol. IV p30.

9 Ibid. Vol. IV p50.

10 Ibid. Vol. IV p56.

11 Ibid. Vol. IV p50.

12 Ibid. Vol. IV p64.

13 Ibid. Vol. IV p66.

14 Ibid. Vol. IV p72.

SIR JOHN SOANE, ARCHITECT

If the arrival of the 30-year old John Soane (**3:1**) at Letton was a significant event for Brampton Gurdon Dillingham it was no less significant for Soane himself. It was to be his first full-house commission from which he went on to become Architect to the Bank of England, to be Professor of Architecture at the Royal Academy, and to rank as one of Britain's finest architects.

He had not had a particularly auspicious start. He was born in 1753 as plain John Soan (without the 'e', which he added later), the youngest son of a bricklayer in Goring-on-Thames. His rise to professional eminence was very much the result of his own hard work and determination to succeed; he learnt the basics of draughtsmanship by being apprenticed to George Dance at the age of 15, staying with him for four years.

It was at this time that a new 'Academy of the Arts' was being established involving study of 'Anatomy, Perspective, Sculpture and Architecture'. It gained the patronage of King George III to become the Royal Academy, and was to play a very significant part in Soane's career. He first won a Silver Medal in 1772 for a 'measured drawing' and after joining Henry Holland in another young architect's practice, went on to win the Gold Medal in 1776 at the age of 23.

THE GRAND TOUR

The Royal Academy's most glittering prize was its travelling scholarship endowed by the King; this provided an opportunity of studying abroad, otherwise denied to all but the sons of wealthy families travelling on the Grand Tour. Soane competed and won, and set off in March 1778 for a two-year journey, which was to have a profound effect on his career as an architect; the experiences he gained were to colour the rest of his life, and could be said to mark the start of his professional career.

During his travels, which were almost entirely in Italy, he visited and studied and sketched countless buildings and building methods, and used these in his later work. But even more important, from Letton's point of view, was his use of the tour to make friends and contacts who would help him obtain clients in the future.

The first of these was the Bishop of Derry, afterwards to become Earl of Bristol, who was a noted patron of the arts, spending a lot of his time in France and Italy. He returned to Ireland regularly, but 'at no time did he allow his pastoral duties to interfere with his pursuit of the arts in general…' [1]. He appeared to John Soane to hold out all sorts of promise for future commissions but at the end of two years, despite Soane spending several weeks at his house and carrying out a number of small schemes for him, nothing significant materialised.

Thomas Pitt however, one of the young men in the 'court' of the Bishop, and one with whom Soane spent a considerable amount of time, became a close and lifelong friend; he was of considerable help in future commissions and may even have been instrumental in introducing Soane to Brampton Gurdon Dillingham.

3:1 John Soane, the architect of Letton Hall, painted by CW Hunneman in 1776 when Soane was 23 years old. He first came to Letton seven years after this.

Another Norfolk contact on the Grand Tour was John Patteson (**3:2**), two years his junior and a member of a well-known Norwich family. He was already talking commissions with Soane, as he writes to his mother:

'Rome 12th April 1779

I am going to take a tour of Sicily in the Spring. Our party consists of five in which number is a very clever Physician and an Architect... the architect whom I mentioned to be of our Sicilian party is a young man whose abilities gained him the Premium of the London Academy and who is now on his studies here with a Pension from our King. If ever you should see him, you will like him I am certain. We have been talking over Plans for you viz: To give you two rooms in Front, 23 or 24 by 18, but in a few posts you shall have the Draughts in small...' [2]

Soane met others in these years who obviously liked him and who became good and loyal friends through the rest of his life, although he was not always an easy person. John Summerson gives us this sketch.

'What of Soane, the man? He was tall and thin, with dark hair, a pale, narrow face, nervous eyes and a small womanish mouth; a striking Physiognomy, not immediately likeable and with an air of withdrawal. A difficult man? Unquestionably; indeed, his memoirs and correspondence show beyond dispute that he was a paranoiac. Constitutionally disposed, no doubt, to this tragic disorder, it seized him of his first disappointment at the hands of the Bishop of Derry after his return from Italy and tortured him more or less incessantly. His happiness was only such as he could wring from a jealous and hostile world – a world over which fortune permitted him a bitter sort of triumph.' [3]

3:2 John Patteson, whose home was in Norwich and who was a fellow traveller with John Soane on the Grand Tour.

BY COURTESY OF NORFOLK MUSEUMS SERVICE

This may seem a little harsh, but he was certainly a man driven by a sense of unjustified persecution, often unable to count up the blessings in his life. The judgement of his students seems to be that he was a hard taskmaster but always fair and often wonderfully generous. He had an enormous capacity for work and no doubt expected the same output from others. Physically he was energetic, often walking ten mile round trips from his London house, and it is not surprising that his health suffered from time to time. This extract from a kind letter from Thomas Pitt shows the type of high regard and concern his friends had for him. It is in reply to a letter from Soane in which he makes a brief reference to feeling unwell.

'I am griev'd my dear Soane that you continue so ill and do not doubt that the vexations of your mind greatly increase your distemper. We shall be extremely glad if you'd try the air of Petersham which we very much hope may be of service to you. There is a little green bed in a room adjoining to the steward's room which has been the best air'd and the most comfortable we always use when we come down. This apartment we recommend to you by all means not as the chearfullest but a great deal the most comfortable.' [4]

SOANE FAMILY LIFE

When John Soane first visited the old Letton Hall he was a bachelor. During the year or so that it took to prepare and agree drawings, he had met Elizabeth Smith(**3:3**), the 23 year old niece of George Wyatt, with whom Soane had dealings in connection with supplying stucco. On the 21 August 1784 they were married, the month after work on the new Letton Hall foundations had began. Soane arrived back in London from Norfolk on the Wednesday before, carried out a few business chores, married at the weekend, and was off again on his architectural rounds on Monday…

It is difficult not to make comparisons between what is written down of the intense and extravagant courtship of Mary Bedingfield by Brampton Gurdon Dillingham, with what is written of John Soane and Elizabeth Smith. Dorothy Stroud has collected together some references from Soane's papers. There was obviously a strong attraction between them but also, on Soane's part, a rather cold concentration on things such as the price of theatre tickets.

3:3 A miniature portrait of Mrs Elizabeth Soane (née Smith).
BY COURTESY OF THE TRUSTEES OF SIR JOHN SOANE'S MUSEUM

'By 10 January 1784 he was taking her to the theatre, noting 'expenses 10/6d', and on 2 March she was dining with him in Margaret Street in company with Mr and Mrs Cooke, when he paid six shillings for wine, 8/6d for sundries and an extra five shillings to the serving maid Betty. Two days later he was taking tea with the Cookes where he found Wyatt and his niece, although for some unspecified reason he was 'damnably vex'd'. On 6 March he noted that he had again escorted Miss Smith to the theatre, and during the next four months the normally brief entries about work in the note books are interspersed with references to dining or supping with 'Eliza' at their respective homes, or visits to Vauxhall or the theatre, the latter being of particular interest to both. Another note records that on 6 May they went to sit for 'sketches by George Dance', and although Soane does not mention at what point their engagement officially began, it must have been recognised, at least by their friends, at this time.

As it transpired, Soane could not have made a better choice of wife, for Eliza was not only endowed with agreeable looks but with intelligence and a degree of patience which was to stand up to fairly rigorous testing until the onset of her last illness… She ran the household efficiently, welcomed the guests and came to be regarded with affection by Soane's friends in all walks of life from the Duchess of Leeds and Lady Bridport to Turner and the ever-impecunious Gandy family.' [5]

With a suggestion of understatement, Dorothy Stroud comments on the new Mrs Soane's feelings when her husband goes off for a business journey just two days after their wedding,

'…leaving Eliza alone to take stock of the new life which lay before her and the realisation that, however sincere her husband's protestations of love might be, she came second to his self-confessed passion for architecture.' [6]

It seems almost as if John Soane regarded his wife merely as someone to inhabit the houses he had designed, and as an extension of his architectural practice; and his two surviving sons (from the four who were born) as products of his drawing board.

His stated ambition was for his sons to continue the architectural dynasty he had founded; and he built perhaps one of his most significant houses Pitzhanger Manor to be the focus of this. But his attempt to control and plan their lives as he might an architectural commission failed painfully. His elder son John might have continued this in some small way had he not pre-deceased his father, but his younger son George turned into a vindictive and abusive man who, in a vicious and critical article condemning 'the Present low state of the Arts in England' – and particularly the work of his father – seemed to have dealt his mother her death blow.[7]

3:4 Sir John Soane's memorial to his wife.
BY COURTESY OF THE TRUSTEES OF SIR JOHN SOANE'S MUSEUM

Eliza Soane died in 1815 at the age of 55, after a long spell of ill health. Soane's notebook was empty for a few days, but resumes with this entry.

> 'Friday – melancholy day indeed! The burial of all that is dear to me in this world and all I wished to live for' [8]

Appropriately, his memorial to her was architectural (**3:4**), and the design of the memorial itself has achieved an immortality of its own in the lines of red telephone boxes.

ARCHITECT MEETS CLIENT

Returning to the start of John Soane's career it is interesting to explore his links with Letton.

The first contact may have come through John Patteson since Brampton Gurdon Dillingham would have known the Patteson family during his time in Norwich. Perhaps Mrs Patteson spoke of the architect who provided plans for her; or John Patteson himself may have had contact with Brampton Gurdon Dillingham through their shared interest as Justices of the Peace.

Soane was carrying out work for Thomas Pitt at Burnham Westgate Hall in North Norfolk and it is possible that this was known. Sir Brampton Gurdon[9], writing several years later says, 'Thomas Pitt… was very intimate with the Gurdon family.' [10]

In whatever way the first contact was made, when Brampton Gurdon Dillingham decided he needed the services of an architect, it was to John Soane he turned.

When the two men met how did they get on together? They were very different personalities; they were to work together quite closely for the next five years, and it was to be thirteen years before the last dealings between them finished. Each one would have brought their own agenda to that first meeting at Letton on 11 July 1783.[11]

For Brampton Gurdon Dillingham it was to be his first work on the family house since his father died four months previously. It has been thought that this July meeting was merely to consider work on the stables, partly because the earliest dated drawings for Letton cover only the stables, but notes sent with Soane's account for the work, indicate the situation of an 'intended mansion' was settled that day.[12] A major decision indeed and one heralding-in a completely new era. It must have needed great courage on the part of Mr Dillingham to decide to replace the house that had been home to his family for many generations. But he had now been married to his second wife for three years, they had a new baby daughter, and this new life really was summoning in a new house.

For John Soane, the three years since his return from Italy July 1780 must have seemed frustrating in many ways. After the major disappointment of receiving no commissions from the Bishop of Derry, there had been several commissions for repairs and alterations but he had not yet been asked to design and build an entirely new house. His work as an architect required this, and he must have been very keen indeed to seize any opportunity that presented itself. Did he sense in his new client a potential willingness to launch out into something completely new? If so, he would have wanted to put all his persuasive efforts into it and make whatever concessions he had to in order to win the commission.

When the commission became his, he had to continue to use all his skill in dealings with his client so that Brampton Gurdon Dillingham and his family would benefit from his skill as an architect. Pierre de la Ruffinière du Prey, in his book on Soane's early work comments on this.

> 'Soane's approach remained fluid, even when he came to publish the Letton design. In his book of 1788, he included plans and elevations 'as built', 'as intended', and 'as originally proposed'. Although these do not vary enormously one from another, none the less they show Soane's continued flexibility and willingness to experiment. Soane was not afraid to display openly the evolution of his ideas. Ultimately, Letton in its finished form demonstrated those subtle areas in which Soane excelled as a country house designer'. [13] (**3:5**)

In addition to dealing with the client himself, Soane also had to cope with comments from the family. The Reverend Peter Forster, Mr Dillingham's brother-in-law wrote to him as follows:

> 'Dear Sir,   [not dated]
>
> I think myself much obliged by your allowing me so much time to look over the elegant design for your house. It has afforded me great entertainment. I shall not however particularise the many things I have to admire in it; it will be to better purpose perhaps to point out such things that may seem to require reconsideration if not altering…' [14]

He then goes on to list a dozen or so points which would be enough to make any architect's heart sink, let alone one with two rejected schemes already under his belt.

Sir Brampton Gurdon quotes what could well have been the family view of Mr Soane at the time…

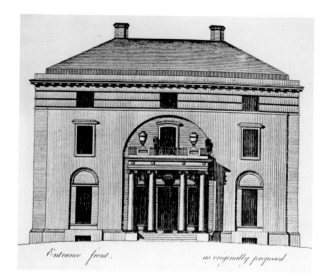

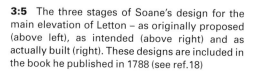

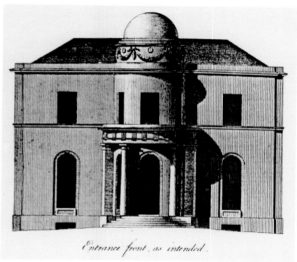

3:5 The three stages of Soane's design for the main elevation of Letton – as originally proposed (above left), as intended (above right) and as actually built (right). These designs are included in the book he published in 1788 (see ref.18)

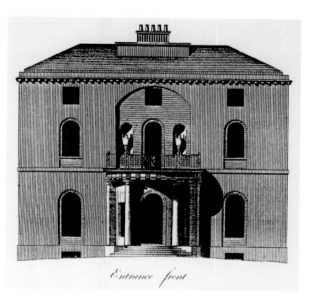

'He returned to England in 1780, and erected several country houses. Being consulted by Mr Gurdon Dillingham with regard to the alterations required to the old Hall, he persuaded him to demolish it, and to build a new house in the so-called Italian white brick style, in which the architect planned so many houses in Norfolk. Sir John Soane's houses are very stoutly built, and exceedingly convenient but they have no beauty being all square in shape with a large bow in the middle, lighted by a skylight.' [15]

Pierre du Prey chronicles fully the stages by which the design evolved and the building worked progressed, until most of it was completed by 1788 at a cost of £6,000. This is the commonly accepted date for the finishing of the house, but Soane was still sending up the occasional drawing, and visiting to check progress, up until the end of 1792. [16]

THE TASK OF THE 18TH-CENTURY ARCHITECT AND BUILDER

There were enormous practical problems to be faced in completing a building project such as Letton in the 18th century.

The amount of detail that Soane put into his plans is most impressive, and it is interesting to see how much he considered was included within his architect's brief. There are for instance, at Letton, drawings of curtain rails (**3:6**), fire surrounds, bookshelf details (**3:7**) as well as the obviously necessary structural drawings of the roof and plans of the drains. To help the client understand these plans he produced beautiful perspective watercolours and a good model, this latter not only for the client but also for use as a visual aid for the workmen and as a three-dimensional tool for the design itself.

Producing the original drawings was only the first step; whenever copies were needed they had to be produced by doing the drawing all over again. Once drawings were completed, they had to be delivered to the client or craftsman by hand, and if there was a query it involved postal delays or yet more travelling.

The architect also took on the role on general contractor. He it was who appointed bricklayers, masons, plasterers etc. As they were all essentially independent craftsmen, it was the role of the architect to ensure that they worked well together, were aware of the timetable and knew the priorities. In the circumstances it was vital to have good and trusted craftsmen on the team, who would co-operate well with each other in between the architect's visits. In the course of completing Letton and the other houses he started in Norfolk shortly afterwards, John Soane built up such a team whose names keep on occurring in the records of different houses.

During the work at Letton, Soane set up his first practice office in London. He now had a handful of people who could help him with on-site measurements, etc., and with the production of drawings. But it was still imperative for the architect himself to visit each site regularly; his reputation was built on keeping costs within budget, completing the building on time and of course 'getting it right'. No matter how effectively he learnt to delegate, the ultimate responsibility was his.

In understanding the workings of John Soane's architectural practice we have a most valuable resource. When he died in 1837 he left the house he had designed for himself at 13 Lincoln's Inn Fields as a museum. It contains his own drawings and papers together with much else; and tucked away in the very heart of this treasure store is a cardboard box containing items that are at one and the same time both simple and ordinary, yet extremely helpful in understanding the work at the time. From the start of his professional career Soane had kept notebooks in which he recorded his daily activities, and these well worn pocket-sized practical notebooks are still available, stored in unassuming little bundles, continuous except for one gap between 1785 and 1788. They are not diaries in the sense of being full of thought and comments, but are nevertheless very effective in evoking the essence of Soane's life and work.

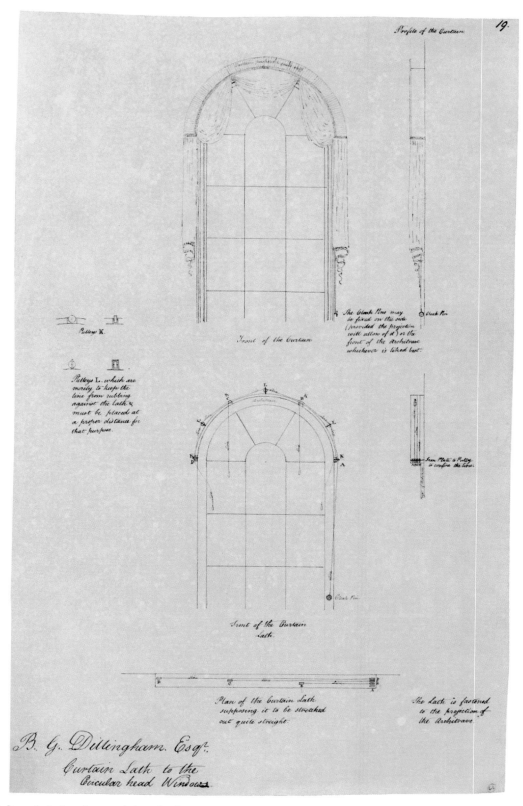

3:6 Soane's designs for curtain hanging for the round head windows – still in use in the present day Drawing Room.

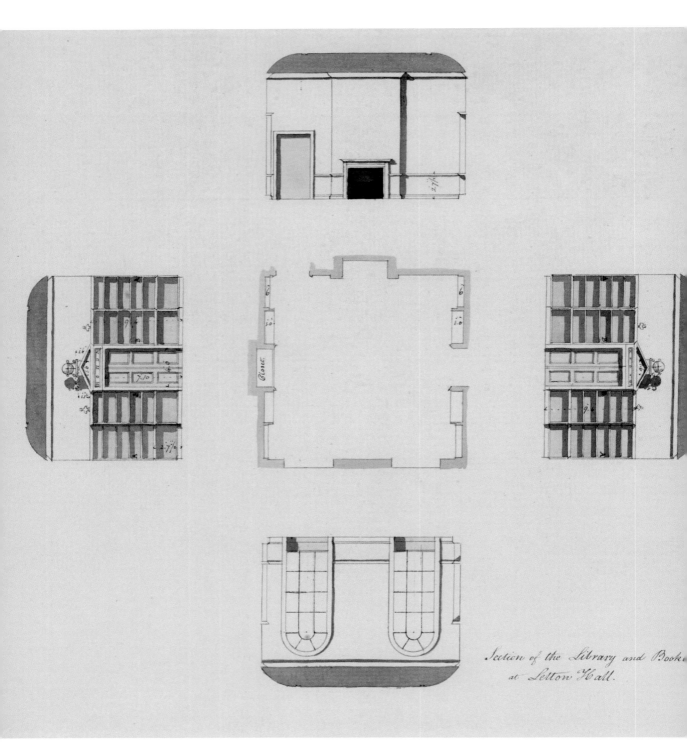

3:7 Designs for the bookcases in the Library. These have been extended and some have been moved since Soane designed them, but are still intact.

These few extracts serve to illustrate the busy pace of his life, and the advance planning that must have been necessary to keep it going. As well as his round of checking and measuring (and the noting down of his expenses) he needed constantly to keep in touch with his clients, discussing progress.

1783				
July 11 Friday	At Letton, seat of B Gurdon Dillingham			
Aug 5 Tuesday	About Mr Dillingham's plans.			
Aug 6 Wednesday	Went on grey mare to Walthamstow about Mr Dillingham's plans			
Aug 7 Thursday	At 3 o' clock to Norwich Six courses on east side of arch tuned.[17]			
Aug 8 Friday	At Norwich, in the afternoon to Mr Dillingham			
Aug 9 Saturday	At Mr Dillingham's with the drawings. Came in the evening in his Phaeton to Mr Collyer. Sent paint, silver button.			
Sept 18 Thursday	Left Mr Pattesons at 8 o' clock and came to Ipswich, Distance about 43 miles.			
		£	s	d
	Diligence and Post'n	0	13	0
	Coachman		1	0
	Breakfast & dinner		4	6
	2 horses to Grundisburgh 6 miles		4	0
	Boy		1	0
	Mr Dillingham's servant		2	0
Sept 19 Friday 20 Saturday	At Mr D, settled plan and on came with Mr D in his chaise to Ipswich and by the Ipswich Coach to London.			
	Coach	£0	19	6d
	Coachman		2	0 d
	Breakfast		1	0 d
	Dinner and C		3	0 d
	Coach		1	0 d

3:8 A page from one of John Soane's notebooks detailing one of his journeys to Letton.

BY COURTESY OF THE TRUSTEES OF SIR JOHN SOANE'S MUSEUM (SM SNB 9P5V-6)

Although he attempted to do most of his travelling in the summer months, occasionally he had to venture out in the depths of winter.

1784	
Jan 21 Wed	Left Norwich and came on Mr Patteson's horses to Dereham. Left the bracelets, Mr C's seal and the miniature and a ring from Mr Wace for Mrs Collyer. From the Collyers to Letton through mountains of snow by the way of Shipdham, arrived at Letton at three in the afternoon.
Jan 22	At Letton settled with the two bricklayers to build the garden wall and stables, Butcher and Spragg. Left Letton at 12 o' clock and came in a most terrible day and by dangerous roads to Fakenham. Left Mr P's servant and horse there and took a guide to Burnham as the snow made it imprudent to risque coming by myself. Came to Burnham Thursday evening 7 o' clock. Gave the guide £0 2s -6d
Jan 24	Left Burnham at 6 0'clock in the morning. No sun scorching, no dust flying but snow quickly falling and hail fiercely driving. Allons donc montez a cheval fers Fakenham. At Dereham gave Mr Collyer a draft for £11-7s -0d being the balance of all accounts between us to Xmas 1783.
April 17 Sat	[At Mrs Patteson's] Mr Day Mr Ever Mr Herring Mr Iselin and Hampton Breakfasted with Mrs Patteson and settled ironwork for the back front of house. Dined at Mr Dillingham's and came to Letton in the evening.
Sunday April 19 [sic]	Wrote to Lord Camelford Miss Smith Mr Lewis Foxhall At church
Monday April 19	Settled foundation of garden walls. Plan of a waggon house The old house to be changed into stables. The new house to be begun in three weeks. Dove came over to receive his directions. Met Mr Preston, a shrewd sensible man, has travelled. Disappointed at Venice, pleased at Vicenza. Dined at Letton.
Tuesday April 20	Left Mr Dillingham at 1 o'clock and came with his horses to Mr J.R. Dashwoods at Cockley Cley near Swaffham.

And so on, day after day throughout the year, and encompassing all Soane's projects and possibilities.

THE NEW LETTON HALL

In 1788 Soane published a book of drawings and details describing several houses he had designed in Norfolk, Suffolk and elsewhere.[18]

This book was obviously intended to publicise his work and was therefore a 'sales document', but it is interesting to note what he saw as the purposes behind the design of Letton Hall, and what features he saw as worthy of special mention. (**3:9**)

· L E T T O N · H A L L ·

· T H E · S E A T · O F · B · G · D I L L I N G H A M · E S Q · N E A R · · S H I P D A M · I N · N O R F O L K ·

THE principal ſtory of this houſe is elevated about four feet; the fronts are of white bricks, and the ſteps, columns, cornices, and other decorations are of Portland ſtone.

· P L A T E · VII ·

· THE · PLAN · OF · THE · PRINCIPAL · STORY · AND · THE · ELEVATION · OF · · THE · ENTRANCE · FRONT ·

A FLIGHT of ſtone ſteps leads to the veſtibule, on the right of which is a library, opening into the withdrawing-room, to which the eating-room adjoins; the breakfaſt-room is in the entrance front on the left ſide of the hall, and all the rooms have ſeparate communications; the beſt ſtair-caſe is placed in the center of the houſe, and is of Portland ſtone; and likewiſe the common ſtair-caſe.

    a. Cloſet, arched and ſecured from fire for papers, records, &c.

    b. A ſmall room for the butler's uſe: the offices being on the baſement ſtory, this room was fitted up with preſſes, ſink, &c.

· P L A T E · VIII ·

· THE · PLAN · OF · THE · BASEMENT · STORY · AND · THE · ENTRANCE · · FRONT · AS · INTENDED ·

IT was propoſed to arch the whole of this ſtory, but the idea was changed after the foundations were laid, and the wine cellar only is arched.

    a. b. c. d. Cellars.

    e. Lobby leading to kitchen, houſekeeper's room, &c.

    f. Paſſage to ſervants hall.

    g. Common ſtair-caſe.

    h. Room for cleaning ſhoes and knives, and for the ſervants to dreſs in.

The other rooms are particulariſed in the plan.

· P L A T E · IX ·

· THE · PLAN · OF · THE · CHAMBER · AND · ATTIC · STORIES ·

THE chamber ſtory contains the lady's dreſſing-room and four chambers, with dreſſing-room, cloſets, &c. BETWEEN the principal floor and the chamber ſtory is a mezzanine (under f. g.) containing a water-cloſet, houſemaid's cloſet, a leaded ſink and the water laid on.

THE attic ſtory contains the nurſery, four chambers, two dreſſing-rooms, &c.

    a. Common powdering-room.

    b. c. e. Cloſets.

    d. Sky-light over beſt ſtair-caſe.

· P L A T E · X ·

· THE · PLAN · OF · THE · PRINCIPAL · STORY · AND · ELEVATION · OF · THE · · ENTRANCE · FRONT · AS . PROPOSED ·

· P L A T E · XI ·

· THE · PLAN · AND · ELEVATIONS · OF · THE · STABLE · BVILDINGS · AS · PROPOSED ·

THE ſtables and coach-houſes are built on a plan forming three ſides of a quadrangle, one ſide making part of the wall of the kitchen garden, and the dung is placed in a ſmall incloſed court, immediately communicating with the garden.

    a. Harneſs, ſaddle-rooms, &c.

    b. Coach-houſes.

c

3:9 The descriptive notes to the drawings of Letton in Soane's book published in 1788 (see ref.18).

THE PRINCIPAL STOREY (3:10): Soane emphasises the 'separate communications' of all the rooms, yet the three main ones also interconnect. This would have provided both the privacy needed for the different functions of each room, and also a progressive 'circuit' from one room to the other in keeping with the developing social habits of the time.[19]

The room to the left of the entrance is marked as 'Mr Dillingham's Room' on the plan, but is described as the 'Breakfast Room' in the written details. Perhaps it was both and used as an additional reception room at times. But Mr Dillingham is shown as already having one room of his own in the basement, which may have been regarded as quite sufficient by some members of the household!

THE CHAMBER STOREY (3:10): Soane says in the particulars that this floor provided 'four bedrooms, plus dressing rooms etc'. This is confirmed by the location of the beds on the plan. It is interesting, though, that the largest and perhaps finest room (with a higher ceiling than the others, and an easterly outlook) is marked with a 'b' as a 'closet'. It must have been intended to be used in conjunction with the bedroom beyond it (through the passageway marked 'c') as a first floor sitting room. Most people in recent times have used it as the principal bedroom, thus making the hall a five-bedroomed house.

The mention of an mezzanine ('under f.g.') with 'the water laid on' is interesting. In Soane's accounts submitted to Mr Dillingham, he includes an amount of £11 6s 3d for a Water Closet from Mr Bramah. Joseph Bramah[20] patented his device only in 1778, so for one to be included in Letton in 1785 was advanced technology indeed. Earth closets are shown elsewhere for the servants.

The skylight over the 'best staircase' was a feature that Soane considered worthy of mention. Sophisticated natural top lighting became a speciality of Soane's designs as his architectural style developed over future years. It was more of a novelty then than it would appear today, and it was certainly expensive at '£20 1s 6d'. [21]

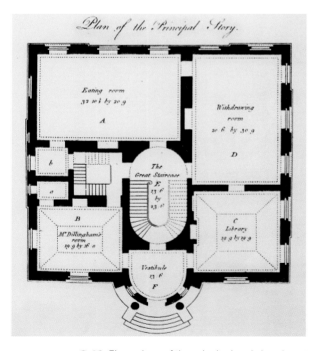
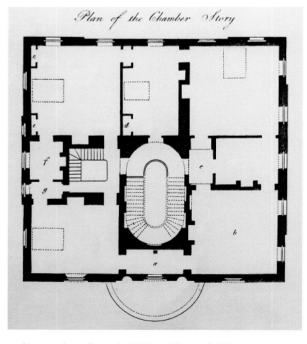

3:10 Floor plans of the principal and chamber storeys of Letton, from Soane's 1788 book (see ref. 18).

LETTON HALL.

Plan of the Attic Story.

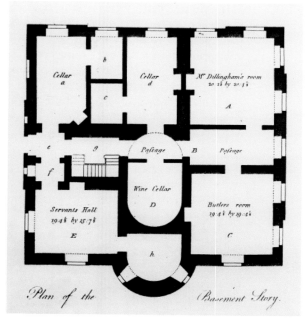

Plan of the   *Basement Story.*

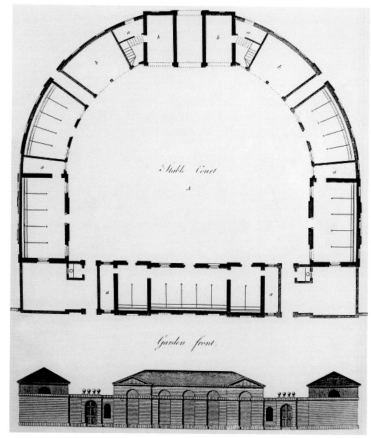

Stable Court

Garden front.

3:11 (Above) Floor plans of the attic and basement storeys of Letton, from Soane's 1788 book (see ref. 18).

3:12 Soane's design for semi-circular stables which although never built were included in his 1788 book (see ref.18).

43

THE ATTIC STOREY (3:11): This floor could only be reached by the 'common staircase' which at this point is narrow and quite steep. It is intended as 'common to all floors' and not merely for 'the common people' (a present-day interpretation by some). Soane has obviously given thought to making the rooms on this floor attractive, with fascinating curved walls in two of them; in fact the rooms are as spacious in floor area as those on the floor below and with lower ceilings are rather more 'liveable-in' by modern standards. It seems likely they were originally intended for young Mary Dillingham's nursery and perhaps even for the three teenage boys.

THE BASEMENT STOREY (3:11): This is not a completely underground cellar level but, due to the four foot elevation of the principal storey, has natural lighting. Thus 'Mr Dillingham's Room' is rather more habitable than would appear at first sight. It is also situated between the wine cellar and the beer cellar, within easy summoning distance of the butler's room, and about as far away from the rest of the family as it is possible to get. It seems rather a strategically-based 'den'.

THE STABLES (3:12): The semi-circular stables shown on the plan in Soane's 1788 book were never built, and are described as '*proposed*' in the written particulars. Presumably Soane included them because he considered them to be a feature that might appeal to other prospective clients. The question of what stables were actually built, when, and by whom is explored later.

However, there is an interesting environmentally-sound feature mentioned by Soane which does exist at present (leaving aside the question of when it was built). He says 'the dung is placed in a small enclosed court, immediately communicating with the garden'. It can be seen from what remains of the structure that this 'court' was at a lower level than the stables so that the dung, when it was tipped in, was conveniently at 'gardeners'-wheelbarrow-height', thus ready for easy distribution. A very sound scheme.

THE OFFICES: There is no mention at all in Soane's book of 'the offices' for Letton, apart from a brief reference on the Basement Storey plan to a semi-underground passage to the kitchens. It was presumably a selling feature for his prospective clients that one didn't even have to know the domestic offices existed, let alone be able to see them.

PROBING BEHIND THE PLANS

Plans don't always tell the whole story. Even in Soane's 1788 book. he admitted of uncertainty over on-site changes as, for instance, in the notes to 'The Basement storey'; 'It was proposed to arch the whole of this storey' he said 'but the idea was changed after the foundations were laid.'

The drawings of 'the offices' are another case in point. Although Soane never published them, there are in fact many drawings showing kitchens, scullery, laundry, brew house, bakery, food store rooms, fuel store rooms and servants bedrooms in different configurations and in different locations (**3:13, 3:14**). Because these areas were of socially lower profile than the main house they attracted less formality and more sketchy drawings; thus a certain amount of probing behind the plans, and on-site detective work is necessary to decide just what was built where. In the case of the offices, it is fairly clear that Soane built at least the first range of buildings that exist now, even if they have been extended and changed around internally many times since.

So far as the stables are concerned, there have been so many Victorian extensions and additions to them that for years many experts considered that they were not the work of Soane at all. However, more recent 'probing behind the plans' has led to interesting discoveries.

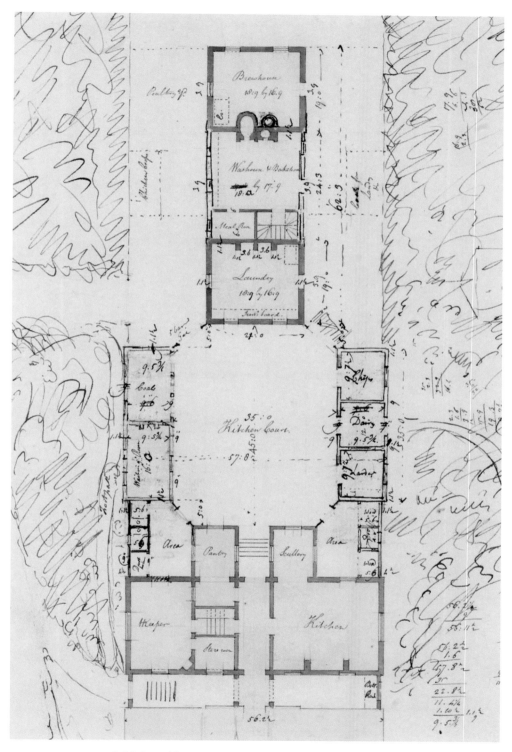

3:13 One of Soane's several designs for the offices at Letton.

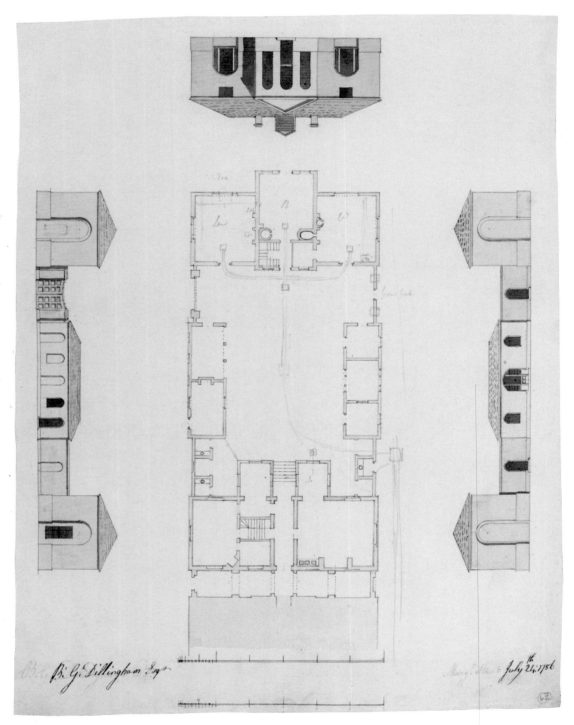

3:14 A further design for Letton's offices, and is the one eventually built. The main change from previous designs is the rotation through 90 degrees of the laundry and brewhouse building, and it is interesting to compare this layout with recent aerial views.

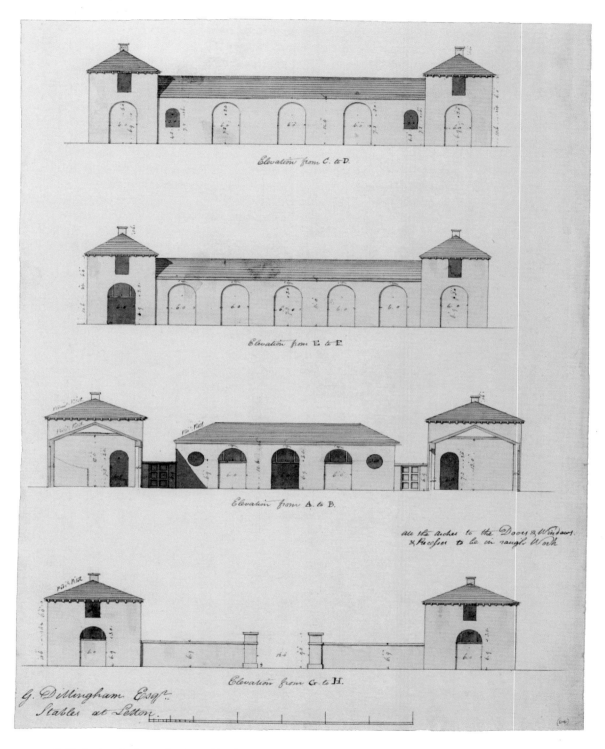

Elevation from C. to D.

Elevation from E. to F.

Elevation from A. to B.

all the arches to the Doors & Windows
& Recesses to be in rough Work

Elevation from G. to H.

G. Dillingham Esq.
Stables at Letton.

3:15 Designs by Soane for the stables that were eventually built. With some interesting changes, these are the buildings that exist today.

The Soane Monuments Trust decided in 1993 to compile a new and revised inventory of the works of Sir John Soane, and awarded a fellowship to Ptolemy Dean to carry out this work. On his visits to Letton he became convinced that at least the garden wall adjacent to the stables was Soanian, and that possibly parts of the stables were too. The out-buildings at Letton are centred on a single axis that runs right through the house, indicating that Soane was creating a kind of 'model estate', including the stables, in this way. Also the blind arches on the rear elevations of the stable buildings, and the carefully-worked brick openings in the walled garden all indicate a Soane touch.

Further searching in the archives, at the prompting of Sir John Soane's Museum, produced a set of drawings (**3:15, 3:16**) that were not with the main ones of Letton. They showed at least two of the stable wings in more-or-less exactly the same form as they exist now, increasing our understanding of the overall plan for the building and of the breadth of work Soane produced.

There have been many other puzzles answered. Did Soane really advertise heroin use in the frieze around his 'Eating Room', which depicts poppy-heads and crossed opium pipes? Answer, yes. It appears in one of his sketches and was a popular design motif of the time (**3:17**).

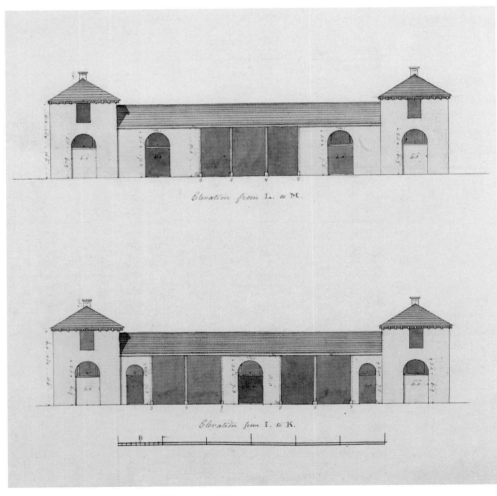

Elevation from I. to M.

Elevation from I. to K.

3:16 Further elevations of Soane's stable designs showing the coach and carriage houses.
BY COURTESY OF THE TRUSTEES OF SIR JOHN SOANE'S MUSEUM (SM 59/148)

3:17 Part of Soane's *Design for Eating Room* at Letton Hall. The poppy head and crossed opium pipe motif can just be made out in the frieze.

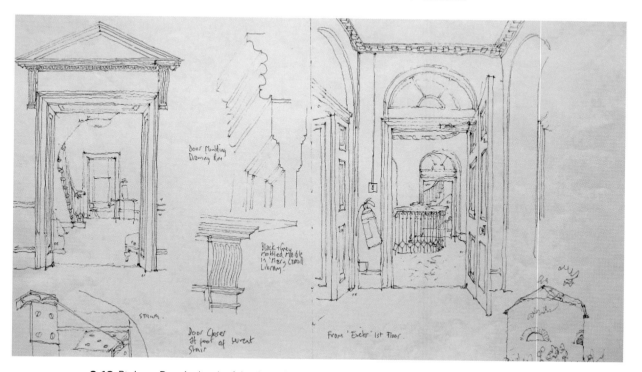

3:18 Ptolemy Dean's sketch of the door closer can be seen at the bottom left of this page from his sketchbook of Letton.

Are the bookshelves in the Library Soanian, even though the room has been extended since? Yes. There is a drawing illustrating them (**3:7**), although there have certainly been later additions. Did he design the two-way weight–operated door closer in the cellar? Probably not, but Ptolemy Dean thought it a fascinating detail so sketched it for further consideration (**3:18**).

We have some of the answers, but there will undoubtedly be more questions in the future, and more reasons to 'probe behind the plans'.

1   Dorothy Stroud, *Sir John Soane, Architect*, de la Mare 1996, p32.

2   Norfolk Record Office, Patteson Intermediate List (1998), Box 12.

3   John Summerson, *Sir John Soane 1753–1837*, Sir John Soane's Museum 1952, p13.

4   Stroud (see 1) p55.

5   Ibid. p56.

6   Ibid. p57.

7   Ibid. p100.

8   Ibid. p100.

9   Sir Brampton Gurdon, a member of the family although not of the Letton line, compiled and commented on many of the Gurdon Papers. See ref (2), previous chapter.

10 The Gurdon Papers Supplementary Volume 1750–1819, pages 36 ff.

11 This meeting is noted both in the Gurdon Papers (see ref.10 above) and also in Soane's notebook for this day. These notebooks are described later in the chapter.

12 The Gurdon Papers Supplementary Volume 1750–1819, pages 36ff. Entry in Accounts for 11 July 1783.

13 Pierre de la Ruffinière du Prey, *The Making of an Architect*, University of Chicago Press, 1982, p288.

14 The Gurdon Papers, Vol. V p12.

15 See 9 above.

16 See ref.13 above, p287 ff.

17 This refers to Blackfriars Bridge in Norwich, which Soane was building at this time.

18 John Soane *Plans, Elevations and Sections of Buildings Erected in the Counties of Norfolk, Suffolk, Yorkshire, Warwickshire, Hertfordshire etc.* London, 1788.

19 Mark Girouard *Life in the English Country House* Yale University Press, 1978. Chapter 7 *The Social House* and Chapter 8 *The Arrival of Informality*.

20 See ref (11) above. The Bramah closet is included as one of the *Bills del'd to Xmas 1787*

21 Ibid. The iron skylight came from Keir and Co.

A NEW HOUSE
FOR THE NEW ERA

It must have been quite an occasion when the family first moved into the new Letton Hall. The house had been rising from the ground across the parkland from the old Hall for nearly five years, from planning to completion. It would have been a talking point and source of interest and preoccupation for all that time. The three Gurdon boys had been teenagers when it started, no doubt keen to climb the wooden scaffolding and explore every new development; but now they were young men.

In 1787, in a legal document assigning a lease [1], Philip the youngest was said to be 'of St John's College, Cambridge', and Thornhagh of 'University College, Oxford'. The oldest son, Theophilus Gurdon was aged 23 in that year, and had set off of his Grand Tour in early 1788. He had no doubt learnt all he could from others who had done The Tour, and had probably discussed it with John Soane too. But his first experiences of the French were even worse than he had feared. In a letter to his father from 'Hôtel de l'Université à Paris, Thursday January 10th 1788' he writes:

> '…I am sure if I could enter into a detail of everything, you could not believe them. The Maids (waiters none), the beds, the filthy dirty brick floors, the knives, tables, in short everything but the linen, which is very nice, was beastly beyond belief; all I can add on this head is that the stories I had heard from Englishmen, which I always thought arose from prejudices, are by no means in the least exaggerated; and their sole aim seems to be in everything to cheat you as much as possible, their ability to accomplish which is considerably aided by the multiplicity and perplexity of their small coin. What do you think of half-a-crown English per night as lodgings for this beastly two-bedded room, in which you sup, and you and your servant both sleep? And three-shillings-and-four-pence for firing, where you do not arrive until nine or ten at night and go by eight in the morning? The wood at the Inns is sold at so much per dog; a common billet such as poor old Jack Cats at Letton, of which it takes a good many to air the room and sheets.' [2]

He kept in mind what was happening at Letton. Writing from Lausanne on 29 July 1788 his comments give an idea of the progress of the building work at home.

> 'I am happy to hear everything at Letton goes on so well. I hope you will soon find yourself comfortably settled, and free from the horrid pest of workmen. Thornhagh has borne his journey very well, is a great enthusiast and will be able to give a very good account. He means to go to England when I go off for Turin, the end of September…I am glad to hear Philip is got to Letton and very well…I feel myself very happy when I think of you at Letton and often wish myself there, where I ever felt myself thoroughly happy. Pray remember me kindly to Mrs G.D. and my Mary.
> Your dutiful son T.G.' [3]

So it looks as if 'moving-in time' was towards the end of 1788. There must have been great excitement as decorations and furnishings were chosen; some furniture was moved over from the old Hall and some new furniture brought in. As the household transferred from old Hall to new, young Mary Gurdon, now aged seven would have been thrilled to move into her nursery at the top the house, looking out over the tops of even the tallest trees.

There was still a great deal to do of course, and John Soane was to continue to visit occasionally, checking work and bring drawings of additions and alterations, for the next four years. His architectural career took a dramatic turn at about the time he finished the main work at Letton when he was invited to become Architect to the Bank of England. His application was supported by the Prime Minister William Pitt, on whose house he had worked at Holwood in Kent. It is interesting to note that the same Thomas Pitt who had helped introduce Soane to Letton was the one who introduced Soane to his cousin the Prime Minister. At the same time as his Bank of England post other commissions arrived including Buckingham House, 10 and 11 Downing Street, Pall Mall, Wimpole Hall etc, making Soane an increasingly well-known name. No doubt the family at Letton Hall watched with interest the upward progress of 'their' architect.

The old Letton Hall had to remain in use until the move, but at that point the plans for its future could be put into action. At least one fireplace was brought over and installed in the butler's room in the basement (where it remained until recent years) Probably many other item were retained, even if only for sentimental value; it had after all been the family house for many generations.

There is no record of what eventually happened to the old house itself, and there is very little trace even of its location now, but PtolemyDean raises the possibility that the bricks may have been used in building the new walled garden [4]. During the planning stages for the new Hall it had been suggested that the old house should be used for stabling but there is no record of this ever happening nor would it seem logical or easy to arrange.

The year after they moved in was to be a busy one for Brampton Gurdon Dillingham, quite apart from his preoccupation with the house. He became Sheriff of Norfolk for 1789 taking up office at the customary time of February in that year. Very little record exists of his term, but from the correspondence of Sir John Venn [5], Sheriff of Norwich from February 1791–2, something of the life can be gleaned. It was an honorary appointment with several duties in the official life of the county, and perhaps Letton first came into its own for official entertaining during Mr Dillingham's term. The post carried with it some patronage, in particular for the sought-after appointment of 'Javelin men'; Sir John Venn was approached by several men claiming that they were 'known to Mr Dillingham'. We don't know his actions but we do know that when the Debtors confined in Norwich Castle write to Sir John asking for money to help them through the 'sevear season' they say the last four sheriffs had helped, and 'Mr Dillingham gave five pounds five shillings'. Obviously he had been a popular Sheriff for some.

As well as duties outside the estate there was still much to do in the grounds around the Hall. Part of the overall plan for Letton was to set out a new park, and the first Road Order had already been passed in 1783. However, in order to protect the parkland around the new Hall, a further Road Order had to be sought. As previously noted, this marked the final demise of the village of Letton (see maps in Appendix I).

Then there was the parkland itself to establish. It appears that Brampton Gurdon Dillingham liked to get involved in this sort of thing personally: in a letter to Sir John Venn dated 27 February 1791 he sends his apologies for not being able to make a proposed meeting 'as I shall want to look around tomorrow, and on Tuesday I have half a hundred trees to plant' [6]. He mentions one or two other things of which it would be interesting to know more, such as 'what track they mean to take in ye Turn Pike Bill' – but the letter is not in good condition and in any case his scrawl is practically illegible. Certain things hadn't changed since the time of his love letters to Mary Bedingfield.

The Letton agricultural estate was in the midst of a period of rapid growth, perhaps assisted by the Dillingham inheritance. Dr Susanna Wade-Martins in her Norfolk survey gives some details.

'By the 1780s the estate consisted of eleven farms and 1286 acres, while by 1838 there were 27 farms and 4498 acres… the family were resident at Letton and much involved in estate improvements. It was almost the only estate to receive a favourable report in the 1861 Norfolk News Survey of 'the cottage homes of England', where the condition of the cottages (about fifty) and the estate were much better than found elsewhere.' [7]

THE FAMILY SEAT

Little is recorded about the house for the first few decades of its existence – but then it was fulfilling its intended role, so perhaps little needed to be said. It had been designed to be a base and focal point for the activities of the squire and his estate, and this is what it was providing.

Looking through the family tree (page 27) at the growing number of Gurdons (the additional surname of Dillingham was only taken for one generation, so all Mr Dillingham's family from now on were Gurdons) it is obvious that the family seat was a busy place at this time. It would also be the time during which the family turned it from merely a house into a home, coming to know it well, finding out their favourite corners and making it their own.

Sadly, one of the first major family events was the death of Philip Gurdon, Brampton Gurdon Dillingham's youngest son. Letton was perhaps then called on to be a haven and refuge for family grief. The memorial tablet in St Mary's Church, Cranworth tells the story:

In memory of

PHILIP BRAMPTON GURDON

Captain in the 58th Regiment of Foot

Third son of B.Gurdon Dillingham esquire

Who after more than a year's severe and perilous service

in the West Indies

During an unparalleled state of sickness in the island

(Under which more than 2/3rds of the army fell,

as well officers as men)

And after the most gallant conduct in the defence of Guadaloupe

And afterwards of Grenada

During the Insurrection raised there

by the Emissaries of the French Convention

Fell by a shot from a brigand concealed behind a rock

At the instant he with a very inferior force

Dislodged the enemy from their post near Pilot-Hill

Took their cannon and completely routed them

He was interred with military honours

At the Observatory near La Vaye in Grenada

where he commanded and died

Universally beloved and lamented by his fellow soldiers and friends

As well as by his father and family

By whose direction this testimony is erected to his memory.

He died 24th April 1795 aged 28.

After Philip's death came a succession of happier events. In 1796 Theophilus (**4:1**) married Anne, daughter of William Mellish of Blyth, Nottinghamshire. It is not clear whether they remained at Letton after their marriage or went to the Norwich Cathedral Close house, as their father had; but a family of six children arrived within a few years, so accommodation would have been a little crowded even at Letton.

There is an indication in the Gurdon Papers that Brampton Gurdon Dillingham moved away from Letton before his death, but he certainly did not do this before his daughter Mary married at the age of 29, on 4 May 1810. This must have been a wonderful family celebration and surely Letton would have been decked out in splendour. She was Brampton Gurdon Dillingham's only daughter and indeed the only child of his second marriage, and at the age of 70 it was an appropriate time to celebrate not only the future of his daughter but also his own full and successful life thus far.

Mary married William Frere who was to become Serjeant-at-Law and Master of Downing College, Cambridge, from 1812–26. Brampton Gurdon Dillingham lived for another ten years but died in March 1829 while at Grundisburgh Hall, another family seat in Suffolk.

It seems that Theophilus was already living at Letton when he inherited the estate, and the Hall continued to be the centre of a busy family life. Over the next few years, four of his six

4:1 Theophilus Thornhagh Gurdon (1764–1849).

PORTRAIT REPRODUCED BY COURTESY OF LORD CRANWORTH

4:2 Brampton Gurdon
(1797–1881).

PORTRAIT REPRODUCED BY
COURTESY OF LORD CRANWORTH

4:3 Mrs Henrietta Susannah
Gurdon (1810–80), daughter of
Lord Colborne.

PORTRAIT REPRODUCED BY COURTESY
OF LORD CRANWORTH

children married; Anne in 1825, his heir Brampton in 1828, the Reverend Philip in 1832 and his son John in 1835.

Theophilus Gurdon himself died in 1849 at the age of 85, his widow Anne dying the following year. Brampton (**4:2**) had married Henrietta Susannah (**4:3**), daughter of Lord Colborne, when she was 18, and their four children were aged between 15 and 20 when the estate was inherited. It had now grown to 4,777 acres. [8]

It must have been during this era, although no records have yet been found, that the first major changes were made to the house as Soane had designed it. Soane had produced a most elegant entrance elevation to Letton (**3:5**) and although the porch that was added is visually unfortunate, on a cold blustery night one can appreciate the practical benefits of additional protection from the Norfolk weather.

THE RAILWAY NEARLY COMES TO LETTON

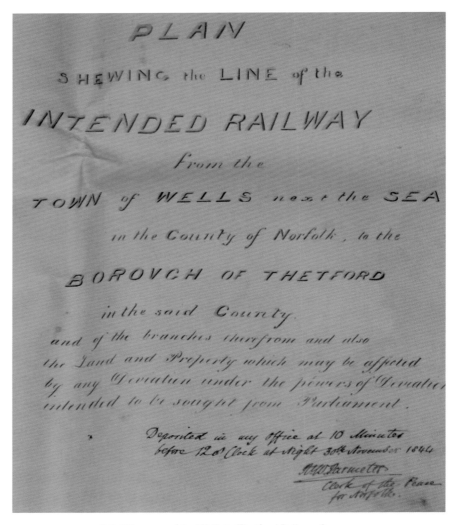

4:4 Title page of the Wells to Thetford Railway Survey.

NORFOLK RECORD OFFICE (C/SCF 310/425)

When the first railway was opened in Norfolk on 30 April 1844 it ran from Norwich to Great Yarmouth and started an era of railway-based development that was to last for around a hundred years. It affected the transport of livestock, coal, general produce and of course people. At that time the accepted way to travel any distance from Letton was to go by carriage for the four miles to Thuxton and then by train to anywhere within the farthest outposts of the empire. But four miles was four miles. How tempting to have a station even closer, and perhaps with even better rail connections beyond. Throughout the county and the country many people were thinking the same thoughts, and so the great rush to improve the rail network began.

One such improvement was the Wells-to-Thetford line. The route was surveyed, and the plans and *Book of Reference* duly submitted (**4:4**). There is an interesting manuscript addition,

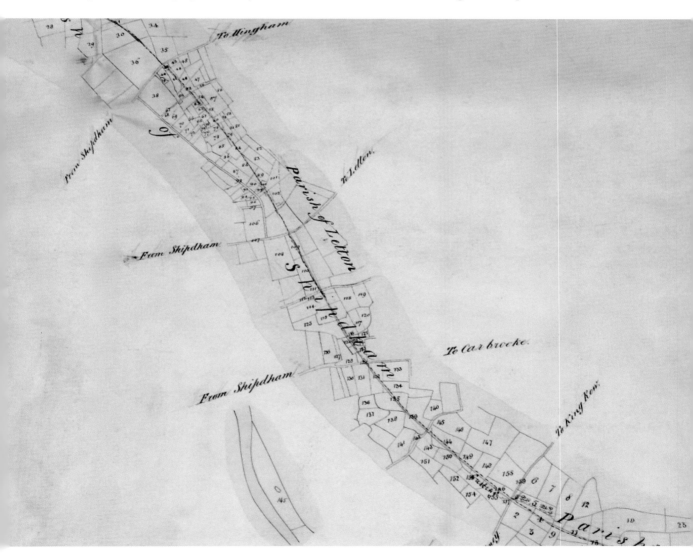

4:5 Part of the Wells to Thetford Railway Survey, showing a plan view of the part adjoining the parish of Letton.

NORFOLK RECORD OFFICE (C/SCF 310/425)

4:6 Map showing the development of railways in Norfolk.
The Norfolk we live in, George Nobbs Publishing, 1975

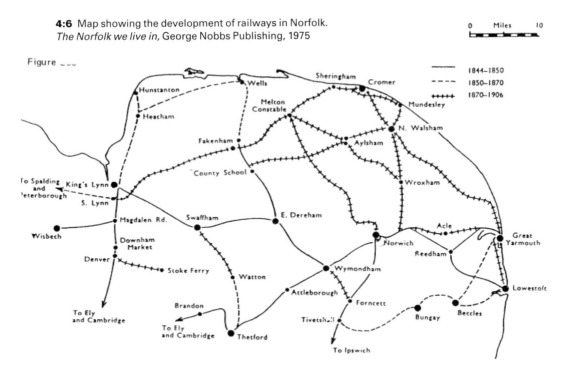

4:7 The Turnpike and Coaching routes in 1840.
The Norfolk we live in, George Nobbs Publishing, 1975

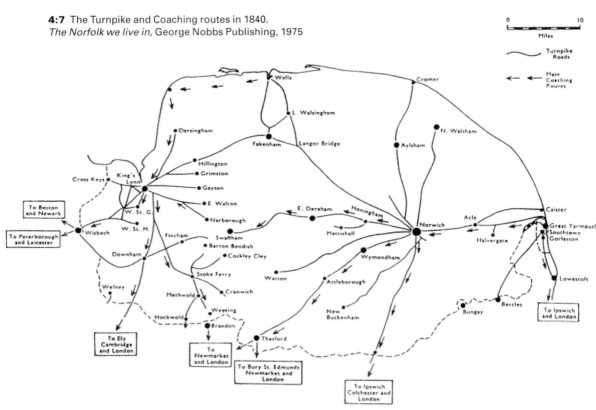

which makes it look as if the applicants were working to a deadline and burning the midnight oil in order to submit the documents:

> 'Deposited in my office at 10 minutes before 12 o' clock at night 30th November 1844
> Signed…
> Clerk of the Peace for Norfolk' [9]

The copy of the survey (**4:5**) shows just how close and convenient it would have been to Letton. Less than half a mile to the line, and no doubt the Railway Company could have been persuaded to provide a 'LETTON HALT' on promise of the estate's patronage.

Study of the map of the railway network (**4:6**) shows there was indeed scope for a line going directly north from Thetford through Dereham and Fakenham to the port of Wells and the north Norfolk coast. But it never happened; there is no record of major opposition to it, so presumably it died a quiet death through lack of commercial interest. It is interesting to note that the Turnpike Map of Norfolk (**4:7**) shows a similar absence of anything directly north out of Thetford so perhaps there was just not enough traffic to justify it.

OUTSIDE THE PARK GATES

Generally, the prosperity of the countryside was rising from the time the new Letton Hall was built, until the agricultural depression set in after the second half of the nineteenth century.

However, this prosperity could take time to filter down to the grass roots. In her Norfolk survey [10] Dr Susanna Wade-Martins reports rents of around £1 per acre in the surviving leases for farms on the estate between 1810 and 1815. In some cases though, even these proved too high for tenants and at least one farmer, William Filby had his assets sold to pay his creditors. The Letton estate had a good reputation for keeping its buildings in good order, but they were of a fairly basic functional standard on all farms except Home Farm.

There was obviously a tension between landlord and tenant as each sought a fair deal for themselves and for their families. An interesting countryside story of Letton has survived, picked out from contemporary press reports and other sources by Michael Carter. First of all he sets the scene by some accounts of living conditions, from the point of view of the agricultural labourer:

> 'George Baldry describes the traditional meal of salt sop, which was 'a few pieces of bread tumbled into a basin with small pieces of butter, lard or dripping, with hot water poured over – the water dipped up out of the river, making our sop like good broth with bubbles of fat floating on top. A few bits of weeds and an insect didn't matter to us, as long as the pangs of hunger were kept at bay'.
>
> He also talks of the pride of the working people, and describes how some old ladies rather than be out of the latest fashion burnt a crust of bread, put it in a cup, filled it with hot water, added a dust of sugar and fancied they were drinking tea.
>
> George Edwards wrote, 'When the Crimean war broke out food rose to famine prices. The only article of food that did not rise to such a proportionately high figure was meat, but that was an article of food which rarely entered a poor man's house, except a little piece of pork occasionally which would weigh about one and a half pounds and this would have to last a family of nine for a week! Very often this small amount could not be obtained – in fact it can be truly said that in those days meat never entered my fathers house more than once or twice a year!" [11]

The tenant farmers had their point of view too, comparing the paid work output of the labourer when working for the farmer with the output when they were working for themselves on their own strip of land.

'...Farmers objected 'I have had men, who when working at days wages work as slowly as possible, and husband their strength doing more in two hours on their allotment afterwards than they have done for me during the whole day.'

A farmer told Frederick Clifford 'Harvest hours are from five until seven (twelve hours actual work); summer ordinary hours six till six (ten hours actual work); winter hours, seven or seven-thirty till four-thirty or five (eight hours, and often not more than seven hours actual work). We lose time sadly in winter, and farmers who pay, as I do, wet and dry, get very poor value for their money.'' [12]

It would seem however, that farmers had their own way of evening up the balance:

'Farmers also tended to underpay their labourers by use of the truck-system (payment in goods), harvest beer being especially common, and although beer at three-halfpence a pint was not an extravagant beverage, the home and family needed every penny and halfpenny for their necessaries.' [13]

POACHERS

In these circumstances, its not surprising that some men decided on a direct assault on the park gates and took to poaching. It seems though that it wasn't always out of need but sometimes the result of the hooligan element.

'In 1851 the parishes of Letton, Shipdham, Cranworth and their neighbourhood were infested with gangs of poachers, whose proceedings were of a most outrageous character; with parties of ten or twelve young men going about night after night armed with loaded guns in pursuit of game. From all we can learn, their conduct does not appear to have been caused by disaffection on account of the general reduction on the rates of wages, from want of employment, from necessity or revenge but from a determination to procure game at all hazards. They have of late almost cleared the estate of Brampton Gurdon Esquire of game.' [14]

The next step in the developing situation came when the gang indulged in some brazen intimidation tactics:

'Late on Saturday 30th November a body of at least eleven men surrounded the dwelling house of Mr Whitear (Mr Gurdon's gamekeeper) and having examined all the outbuildings where they imagined he might possibly be concealed, they ransacked the whole of his premises without finding him. With bitter imprecations they dared him to come forth, swearing that if he did they would shoot him. Then before leaving they fired off their guns at his house, and the shootings of the assailants were responded to by the dogs on the neighbouring farms for miles around until the whole district was disturbed and excited.' [15]

The squire was not going to stand for this attack on his employee and summoned police support. We now have a blow-by-blow account of their dramatic story, which took place in the woods just across from Letton's lodge:

'On Monday 1st December 1851, Superintendent Parker with about a dozen rural policemen, left Swaffham and proceeded to Letton Park, which is nearly three miles in circuit; and, with the consent of the Norwich Watch Committee, Constable Noller, being a strong powerful man, went over to aid the county police. The police were secreted for a week, watching at night, and while thus engaged they often heard the poachers firing at a distance out of the park. On the bright moonlit night of Saturday 6th December, the police, who were armed ready for an encounter with the ruffians, and the keepers, waited in ambush. Shortly after twelve o' clock the police heard three guns fired off successively in a cover; the party of the Watch and police consisting of fourteen or fifteen men, crossed the road into the wood and went to the far end of it…The poachers seeing them cried 'stand back' upon which Parker turned round and said, 'Come on my boys here they are'. Before Parker could turn around, or the police and Watch stop, the poachers had fired two or three guns at them. Parker being the foremost of the police received the charge of one of the guns full in his face, and fell severely wounded. Constable Greenacre received five shots in the shoulder and face, but was not so seriously hurt, and a tree intercepted the charge of the third gun.' [16]

The pace of the battle hots up; the poachers as well as carrying guns 'were armed with large clubs and made a stout resistance.' Parker cries 'I am shot, go in Greenacre' to one of his constables who goes in and after a chase of 30 yards, knocks down a poacher. PC Rivett despite a gun being pointed at him, knocks it aside and takes another poacher into custody. PC Richard George manages to get handcuffs on another… out on the fringe of the battle another little incident takes place when a poacher offers a five-shilling bribe to his captor. It was not accepted (the newspaper says) but the poacher escaped never-the-less, at least for a while. Two men are chased to their house but 'soon taken there, from their beds. All of them were in disguises and had their faces blackened, so that if seen they might not again be recognised'.

All those captured are hauled straight off to the local magistrate – although it does seem that the scales of justice are rather weighted against them when the magistrate turns out to be the squire's brother.

> 'On the same night the five prisoners were taken before the Reverend P. Gurdon and after a short examination they were remanded and sent to Norwich Castle'. [17]

The episode was not without cost to the police however.

> 'After the affray superintendent Parker was conveyed to his home at Swaffham, where the surgeon Mr Whitting attended him and removed twenty-five shots of number five size from his face and neck.' [18]

Altogether seven young men ended up in custody. Their names were Richard Lincoln (19), William Hunter (20), William Stagg (27), John Lake (21), Robert Buckle (19), William Harwood (19) and John Hunter (21). They were not sentenced until two months or so later, and the sentences were harsh. Lincoln, W. Hunter and Harwood were transported for ten years; Buckle, Stagg and J. Hunter imprisoned for two years with hard labour. John Lake was discharged, due to insufficient evidence against him.

The reaction to the incident is interesting. The neighbourhood seemed generally relieved.

> 'Such a fight has caused the greatest excitement in the surrounding villages. The capture of these fellows, all of whom are well-known old offenders is regarded by the population generally of this locality, with great satisfaction, as they have for several months been compelled to feel that no description of moveable property was safe while they were permitted to be at large; and it is believed that the sheep and poultry stealing and other deprivations so frequent of late, may be placed to the account of some members of this gang which it is hoped will now be thoroughly broken up.' [19]

But reaction wasn't all against the poachers. Squire Gurdon had his knuckles rapped:

> 'The judge agreed that the landlord had no right to employ police who were in that sense like soldiers. They were to obey the orders of their superintendent, and acting under his orders they were justified in what they did. It appeared that they were there for a week and this thing should be guarded against because it was likely to lead to ill will.' [20]

The Council for the Defence naturally came down strongly on the poachers' side and made some good points, which apparently roused sympathy from the community.

'The defence showed signs of disgust that six young men who, if the right love and feeling which the rich ought to show to the poor had been displayed towards them in their youth, would have grown up to be a comfort to their friends instead of being brought there for trial. He remarked that if gentlemen would preserve game they must take the proper means to preserve it, they had no right to employ the police for that purpose (and further), deplored that these young men should be allowed to grow up like so many weeds in the neighbourhood of the mansions of the rich; the care which ought to have been bestowed on them having being lavished on the game of their preserves.' [21]

No doubt it was a very much talked about incident around the dinner tables at Letton, and probably those of neighbouring seats too. It was perhaps a timely reminder that the world 'outside the Park gates' had a life and needs of its own, and could not be ignored. The tall mansion, of creamy white brick, 'standing well' in its estate, must beware of becoming an ivory tower.

1   Norfolk record Office, MC 76/6

2   Gurdon Papers Vol. V, p16.

3   Ibid. Vol. V, p38. This letter forms one of a full and fascinating correspondence, but which is outside the scope of this book.

4   Soane Monuments Trust, Inventory Listing Ref.21, 1996.

5   Norfolk Record Office, Colman MSS, COL/8/104/1-92.

6   See 1 above.

7   Dr Susanna Wade-Martins *Historic Farm Buildings – including a Norfolk Survey*, Batsford, 1991, p101.

8   W. Rye *Norfolk Families* 1913.

9   Norfolk Record Office C/Scf 310/425, Book of Reference and Plans

10 See 7 above, p102.

11 Michael J. Carter *Peasants and Poachers – a study in rural disorder in Norfolk*, The Boydell press, 1980, p40.

12 Ibid. p 44.

13 Ibid. p 44.

14 Ibid. p41

15 Ibid. p41

16 Ibid. p42

17 Ibid. p43

18 Ibid. p43

19 Ibid. p43

20 Ibid. p44

21 Ibid. p44

LORD CRANWORTH
AND THE VICTORIAN YEARS

Robert Thornhagh Gurdon (**5:1**), who was later to become first Baron Cranworth, inherited the Letton estate in 1881, when he was 52, after the death of his father at the age of 84. He was to hold the title for only 21 years until his own death in 1902.

His life spanned Queen Victoria's reign; and although both his father and grandfather held Letton for parts of her reign it seems a good way to chronicle Letton in the Victorian era is to centre on RT Gurdon's life and follow it through. This is partly because of the particular records that have survived, and partly because he fits so well the image of a Victorian gentleman.

RT Gurdon might have expected to inherit the estate for rather longer than he did – for at least 30 years had the family pattern remained consistent – but then families often don't live and die according to pattern, and in his case he died rather younger than the family tradition. Other factors such as second marriages, and large age differences between marriage partners play a part in disrupting patterns, and Letton seems to have had rather a larger share than normal in this area. Of the eight male owners holding Letton within the scope of this book, three entered into second marriages; and the age difference between husband and wife, for four out of these eight, was more than 20 years.

Whether or nor RT Gurdon was cheated of a few years of his inheritance he made sure his years of tenure were full and active ones; nor were his early years before coming into the estate dull and unproductive either, for he seems to have been a man of exceptional energy and vigour.

He was Captain of School at Eton and at Trinity College, Cambridge in 1852 he distinguished himself by being placed among the senior Optimes. He was called to the Bar in 1856 and for a time practised on the Northern Circuit before embarking on a lifelong work of public service in national politics, the Quarter Sessions and Local Government, including becoming the first Chairman of Norfolk County Council. In some of this, he was following his father who had also been an MP for a number of years, and as well had carried out County duties.

In addition to his public work he shared in the overseeing of the estate; the full responsibility for this of course belonged to his father as head of the family until his death, and it is interesting to note examples of this being acknowledged in practice. For instance, in the documents relating to George Forrester who carried out general maintenance work for the estate from 1873–1901, Mr Forrester clearly addresses his reports and accounts 'George Forrester in account with Brampton Gurdon Esquire' right up until the latter's death at the age of 84 [1]. Only then does it change to 'Robert Thornhagh Gurdon Esquire'. But one can imagine that in the later years at least, the son would have kept an eye on what was going on, even if only to be prepared for what he would be taking on when he inherited.

5:1 Robert Thornhagh Gurdon (1829–1902). Created 1st Baron Cranworth 1899.

PORTRAIT REPRODUCED BY COURTESY OF LORD CRANWORTH

THE REVEREND BENJAMIN ARMSTRONG

A rich source of information on life at Letton through the Victorian years is the diaries of the Reverent Benjamin Armstrong (**5:2**), who was vicar of East Dereham (six miles from Letton) from 1850–88. His comments on the times have proved both popular and informative and there have been at least two volumes of extracts published; his chronological entries take us through life at Letton over the period, spanning the lives of both RT Gurdon and his father.

After serving two curacies and as vicar of Little Stanmore, Middlesex, he came prepared for Dereham to be his life and ministry for the foreseeable future. He aimed to be a good parish priest for his people, to care for them, to educate them and help them deepen their faith.

He also held strongly to the ideals of the Oxford Movement and in his high church stance had a very uneasy relationship with his mainly low church bishops. His desire to restore certain rituals and practices into parochial worship also led him into regular conflict with several of his parishioners; his diaries are therefore sometimes preoccupied with a sensitivity over, for instance, where his fellow priest stood to celebrate Holy Communion, or over clergy dress or over the place of music in the services. The introduction into the congregation of 'Hymns Ancient and Modern' in 1864 was a major issue, as was the introduction of a weekly sacrament. Somehow, even the installation of gas lighting in the church, and later on a measure of central heating, became issues charged with heavy overtones of religious and ecclesiastical politics.

But nevertheless his diaries offer an unadorned historical record of life in his times, and make a very good read. Those entries which contain references to the Gurdons or to Letton are singled out, leaving them for the most part to speak for themselves. The full entry for each day is selected; but if they give the impression that life for the parish priest of that time was a succession of dinner parties, this is a little unfair taking the diaries as a whole. It is merely that it was on these occasions that he had his most noteworthy contact with the Gurdons.

> '*August 20th 1852*: Dined with Mr and Mrs [Brampton] Gurdon of Letton. They are people of great style and the lady is the daughter of Lord Colborne, who is staying there. Lord and Lady Colborne are very agreeable people, but as is generally the case among grandees, no opportunity presented itself for intellectual converse. The mansion at Letton is beautifully furnished and the entire dinner service was of silver. The Gurdons are good church people although Whigs in politics. The son [RT Gurdon] has recently distinguished himself at Cambridge and a brother of Mrs Gurdon is incumbent of four livings near Dereham'. [2]

> '*October 8th 1853*: Dined with the Gurdons of Letton Hall and enjoyed an evening enhanced by many attractions. One is loath to leave where wealth, taste, family and accomplishments lend their combined aid.' [3]

> '*January 3rd 1854*: [included a propos of the above] In the evening went to a party at Mr Anfrere's. Very slow – small rooms, piano out of tune, bad wine and stupid people. Still, we think it right to go to such parties and it is a satisfaction to feel that one is giving pleasure at a moderate cost of self-denial.' [4]

> '*February 8th 1854*: Dined at the Lee Warners and met the Keppels, the Gurdons, Mr Pratt, Mr Haggard and others. Mr Gurdon said that when he frequented 'Brooks's' [5] they used to be playing cards all day as well as half the night at £40 the rubber, which was not considered high. Now there is very little playing even in the evening, and that restricted to ten shillings and 6d points. High enough too!' [6]

> '*February 7th 1855*: Affairs in the Crimea most wretched. The government at home is broken up and reconstructed. Lord Palmerston is premier, and the Duke of Newcastle, Lord Aberdeen, and Lord John Russell retire from the Cabinet. Half the town laid up with influenza. Took my little girls to a concert party given by our organist Mr Martin. I was amazed to see how humbug was reigning supreme.

5:2 Reverend Benjamin Armstrong, Vicar of Dereham 1850–1888

Thus, the giver of the concert stars himself 'Professor Martin', and 'Herr Rust' of 'Her Majesty's Private Band' is non other than plain Bill Rust, whose father shoes horses and whose mother sells cakes and fruits. He is said not to be connected with Her Majesty except as a private and loyal subject. Then there was Lieutenant H, the ci-devant Guardsman, twisting his moustache to Miss LW whose heart he is unable to subdue; and there was young Mr G, the lawyer*, improving the occasion with pretty Miss R...I believe that half the people thought the music (which was very good) was a consideration quite secondary to their own little plans'. [7]

*Another reference to RT Gurdon, who was to be called to the bar the following year. But the 'pretty Miss R' was not to be his wife.

'August 14th 1855: Dined at the Gurdons, surrounded by all that wealth and good taste could suggest. Evening diversified with music and singing. The Edwardes of Hardingham and the Johnsons of Yaxham were the only people whom we knew, the party mainly consisting of people staying in the house'. [8]

'January 1st 1857: Dined at Letton Hall. Everything refined and beautiful – powdered flunkies, silver plate, rare exotics and all that kind of thing. On our way we saw a planet so close to the moon as almost to touch it. This was an occultation of Jupiter, which passed behind the moon and reappeared on the other side in about an hour's time.' [9]

'April 6th 1859: The heat oppressive and everything a month before its usual time. It seems as if we are going to return to the Poets May. Mrs Gurdon, the wife of our MP [Brampton Gurdon, then representing West Norfolk] writes a seductive letter to ask me to vote for her husband, as Parliament is dissolved in consequence of Lord Derby's government being unable to carry the Reform Bill. Must decline, however, and I shall adhere to the plan that I hitherto have followed of not voting at all.' [10]

'August 16th 1859: Lunched with the Adlingtons* and joined in the new French game of croquet. It is a sort of lawn billiards played with a long handled mallet. The Gurdons who had called on us the day before, called and joined in.' [11]

*The Adlingtons of nearby Holme Hale Hall. See note following the entry for 15 September 1869.

'September 18th 1861: Our darling Helen accompanied us to her first dinner party at Letton Hall. We were glad her debut should be made at so good a house, and where the kindness and unaffected simplicity of the inmates contrasts so favourably with the would-be genteel. Among the guests were Hon. Admiral Eden, Hon. and Mrs Delavel Astley and the Adlingtons.' [12]

'January 2nd 1862: To Norwich on business. Mr [Brampton] Gurdon MP in the carriage who said that the final answer from America will come on the 5th inst. which will determine whether we are to have peace or war.' [13]

'October 6th 1862: The town much shocked at hearing that Mr Lombe [of Bylaugh Hall, Dereham] is dead. They say that he has not made a will. Poor Madame will return to Paris. It is a sad end to a courtship of sixteen years. But while the Lombes are in grief on one side of us, the Gurdons on the other side are at the height of festivity. Their son has brought his bride to Letton on a visit. They were met by the tenantry, who dragged in their carriage. We called there today and missed them through their having come to call on us.' [14]

Mr Robert Thornhagh Gurdon had married Harriet, a daughter of Sir William Miles on 4 September a month earlier, when she was 26 and he was 33.

They were not living at Letton but were probably in London at their house at 5 Portland Square. They were to have a daughter, Amy, about 18 months later, but sadly Mrs Harriet Gurdon died shortly after the baby was born. RT Gurdon was to marry again, but not for another ten years; no doubt he remembered the similar experiences of his great great grandfather Brampton Gurdon Dillingham.

'*September 22nd 1863*: A grand entertainment to the Dereham and Wymondham Volunteers at Letton Hall. A vast crowd was assembled. An elegant repast was provided for the guests in the dining-room and the volunteers, about 150 in number, sat down to an excellent dinner under a tent. The speeches were unusually good, especially those of Lord Wodehouse and Robert Gurdon, who is captain of the Wymondham Corps. Captain Bulwer replied for the Derehamites'. [15]

'*July 10th 1865*: Dereham in a great state of excitement at the result of the election, our friend [Brampton] Gurdon (Liberal) being ousted by a conservative. East Norfolk has done the same. I hear there have been great rows at Swaffham and Fakenham. A conservative supersedes Gladstone at Oxford.' [16]

'*May 31st 1867*: [The Armstrongs were on one of their regular visits to London, where they had visited the Royal Academy, been to 'a melodrama' at Drury Lane Theatre and visited the Horticultural Show in Regents Park – where the dresses of the ladies apparently were the 'chief feature'.] Took my younger daughter to see the crowd in Rotten Row. There were several Norfolk Grandees there – Lord Leicester, Lord Sondes, the Hon. D. Astley, Mr and Mrs R Gurdon and others.' [17]

The reference here to 'Mrs R Gurdon' is interesting, The first Mrs Gurdon had died three years previously and he wasn't to marry Mary, his second wife, until 1874 in seven years time. It could be a diary slip, or he could be referring to Mr and Mrs B[rampton] Gurdon.

'*September 15th 1869*: Took my wife and elder daughter to dine with the [Brampton] Gurdons at Letton. Considering the deaths of both daughters and daughter-in-law and political defeats of father and son it seemed wonderful to dine here again as if nothing had happened.' [18]

Mr Gurdon, senior, had lost the West Norfolk constituency in 1865 and RT Gurdon had unsuccessfully contested North Norfolk in 1868. The daughter-in-law referred to was of course RT Gurdon's wife, Harriet. Their younger daughter, Amy Louise, had died unmarried five years ago in 1864.

The Gurdons' other daughter Charlotte had married Horace Broke, son of General Broke, some years ago, leading to a continuing local link between the Brokes and Letton. Horace Broke was a barrister so perhaps had met Charlotte through her brother RT Gurdon, a fellow barrister. Sadly Charlotte died on 11 January 1868, the final misfortune to which the diary refers.

Major General Robert Broke of Holme Hale Hall remembers that both his parents and grandparents had romantic associations with Letton. His father, the Reverend Horatio Broke, was curate in Dereham in 1892 (a few years after the Reverend Benjamin Armstrong's time as vicar) and had come to Letton, probably on foot, for a garden party. Miss Mary Campbell Adlington, then age 21, had been driven over in the Landau from Holme Hale Hall. The two met for the first time on the lawns of Letton and a year later were married.

'*April 5th 1870*: The Ruridecanal Chapter was held at Dereham as there was no apartment at Yaxham big enough for the purpose. The question was 'Aye or No' as to whether there should be a Diocesan Conference. The debate was opened by RT Gurdon Esquire. The 'Ayes' carried it nem. con., one clergyman and six laymen not voting at all.' [19]

'*April 14th 1871*: The day of the election of a member for South Norfolk, in consequence of the death of Mr Howes, our late Member. The candidates were Sir R. Buxton (C) and our old friend Robert Gurdon of Letton (L). As I told Mr Gurdon Senior, it was a great struggle between personal regard and public duty to vote against his son, but in these days, when the Liberals are doing so much to undermine the church, there is no help for it. Both candidates are unimpeachable in character, but such is the power of personal influence that at <u>Dereham</u> the Liberals got a majority on account of Letton being in the vicinity. An immense pressure was exerted, but the Conservatives won the <u>election</u> by 370 votes.' [20]

This election was the second that RT Gurdon had contested unsuccessfully. He was to contest seven more elections, some successfully others not, before entering the House of Lords. [21] He had also recently been appointed Chairman of the Norfolk Quarter sessions, a role in which he was to continue until 1901, thus following two parallel avenues of public service.

'*October 5th 1871*: Dined at Letton Hall. It was the more kind of the Gurdons to ask us after my voting against their son at the last election.' [22]

'*October 24th 1872*: To the Diocesan Conference at Norwich. Subject: 'Church Defence and Church Reform'. Very good papers by Robert Gurdon and the Reverend Mr Collett, but the layman's by far the better of the two. In the afternoon session papers on education were read by Sir F. Buxton and the Reverend Mr Cooper of Forncett. Here the order was reversed, the clergyman's paper being far superior to the layman's…' [23]

'*December 4th 1873*: Dined at the Gurdons of Letton. Met among others Mrs Ross, the winner of the great International Rifle Prize. Nothing interesting in the conversation.' [24]

After the end of 1873 there are virtually no references to Letton or the Gurdon family in the published extracts from the Reverend Armstrong's diary until around 1880. Brampton Gurdon was now 75 years old and possibly he and his wife were entertaining less.

RT Gurdon also had other preoccupations. On the 27 July 1874 he married Emily Frances (**5:3**), third daughter of the Reverend Robert Boothby-Heathcote of Friday Hall, Chingford, Essex. He was 45 years of age and his bride was 24. A little under a year later their son Bertram Robert was born, but sadly lived only a few weeks. The following year their daughter Muriel Charlotte was born, and the year after that, on the 13 June 1877 a son and heir was born, Bertram Francis Gurdon.

In 1880 there are two more entries in the diaries that give a clue to what was happening not only on the political front, but also in the agricultural world, which of course was the world underpinning the life of the Letton Hall estate.

'*March 19th 1880*: A political day. Dereham being the junction of South and West Norfolk, the candidates for both divisions addressed the farmers at market – viz. Amherst and Bentinck (both Conservative) for the West, and Sir R. Buxton and CS Reade (both Conservative) for the South. An hour afterwards Robert Gurdon (Liberal) for South and Mr Anthony Hamond (Liberal) for West had their meeting. There seems to be an idea that Gurdon may get in, especially as the farmers, being in despair at the bad times, are not satisfied with Mr Reade. Our beautiful lantern tower renovated; it is now quite a picture.' [25]

'*April 7th 1880*: The result of the South Norfolk election was made known, and was the more interesting from one's personal knowledge of all the candidates, and from the closeness of the contest.

Sir R. Buxton only headed R. Gurdon by eight votes, and Gurdon was second by <u>one</u>! Thus C.S. Reade, the once popular tenant farmer MP, who worked so well, and who actually gave up an appointment worth £1,000 per year because he differs from his Ministry on a point which he thought harmful to agriculture, is ousted! [i.e. RT Gurdon was returned for South Norfolk, beating CS Reade, the sitting MP, by only one vote]. The charge against him is that he was gradually aiding the landlords rather than the tenants. But the truth is that the farmers have suffered so severely of late years that they think any change better than none.' [26]

5:3 Lady Emily Cranworth (*née* Boothby-Heathcote) 1850–1934.

PORTRAIT REPRODUCED BY COURTESY OF LORD CRANWORTH

In fact, both the tenant farmers and the landlords had been experiencing difficulties from around 1870 onwards, as the depression in agriculture began to harden. Dr Barnes in her book on Norfolk landowners states 'the 1850s and 1860s had been *the golden years* of agriculture. Prosperity was taken for granted on the assumption that the palmy days would continue indefinitely' [27]. She points out that the population of England and Wales rose from 7.5 million to 26 million between 1781 and 1881, outstripping the resources for home-produced food, and leading to food importation in exchange for exports of coal and manufactured goods.

'The seriousness of the depression was underestimated in its early stages. Initially the downturn was attributed to a series of atrocious summers in Britain throughout the years 1875 to 1879, which caused bad harvests and encouraged disease amongst farm stock'.[28]

But gradually, as tenant farmers felt the pressure and had to delay rent payments, the landlords also began to realise the serious situation. They had no option but to reduce rents or end up with empty and untenantable farms. Dr Barnes quotes examples of rents falling between 25 per cent and 56 per cent over a 20-year period from around 1875 onwards. [29]

Although recovery was eventually to come, the situation had serious and lasting effects on many Norfolk estates, including Letton. But this was not to be apparent immediately. Medium size estates such as Letton, although without the build up of reserves of the really large estates, were better able to weather the difficult times than smaller holdings.

In April 1881 Mr Brampton Gurdon died. There is no reference in the published extracts to record Benjamin Armstrong's reaction to the death of his old friend although no doubt he made private comments. He does refer to one aspect however.

'June 17th 1882: The will of the late Mr Gurdon of Letton, according to the papers, is proved at about £200,000! His wife had large property besides. It must be a fearful responsibility to be possessed of so much.' [30]

RT GURDON INHERITS

When taking stock of his life in 1881, as he inherited the estate from his father, Robert Thornhagh Gurdon could have been well pleased.

– He was master of nearly 5,000 acres. Despite the depression in agriculture, the estate was surviving – and in any case some experts were predicting better times ahead…(quite wrongly as it turned out).

– With the land, he also now held Letton Hall as an appropriate seat for a man of his standing.

– He had at last been elected to Parliament as the Member for South Norfolk, and was to hold it until 1885; his political ambitions were beginning to be realised.

– As a Magistrate, Chairman of the Quarter Sessions, Captain of the 4th Volunteer Battalion of the Norfolk Regiment, he was ably filling his duties in the County.

– He was a relatively young man, at 52, at the height of his vigour. His wife had just turned 30 and he had a son and heir Bertram Francis, aged four. His daughter Amy, from his first marriage, at 17 was at the start of her life as a young lady; and his daughter Muriel was aged five.

It appeared that a whole new phase of life was beginning for him, full of promise for the future. There is tangible evidence, in the form of the surviving fabric of Letton Hall, that he set about this new phase by embarking on a major series of improvements and embellishments to the house that was going to be his family base from now on. The mood of the time was very much that one's status and success should be reflected in the grandeur of one's house:

'Many Halls were renovated or rebuilt during the nineteenth century, partly because life styles changed. The coming of the railway age made estates more accessible, and lavish shooting parties were organised. Each guest would bring his own retinue of staff, so big Servants' Wings were added to accommodate extra servants. New kitchens were added from which were produced the formal dinners of eight courses which were expected on such occasions. The ladies might join the guns for a picnic lunch, but during the inevitable intervals of activity they strolled in the gardens, which were replanned with terracing and balustrading, statues and fountains. No self-respecting Victorian landowner could feel his mission to improve had been accomplished unless he could install or enlarge his lake…' [31]

What is said above for shooting parties would apply also to politically-inspired occasions or for gatherings of local people involved in county affairs. The Brampton Gurdons had obviously carried out their share of entertaining, but as age increased, with Mr Gurdon in his eighties, it was less likely that they would have felt the need to develop the house to keep up with the fashions of the moment. RT Gurdon clearly felt the need to develop; had he been waiting impatiently in the wings until he inherited and could make the changes he felt were long overdue? – or was he merely taking the opportunity, with a certain amount of money available, to update the house as he moved in?

Whatever the reasons, architects were called in (with the first drawings dated some months before Mr Gurdon senior died) and work started very soon. The architects chosen were the Norwich practice of Edward Boardman and Son, who had worked on many Halls and large projects around the county. Drawings and sketches have now been passed by the practice to the Norfolk Record Office. [32]

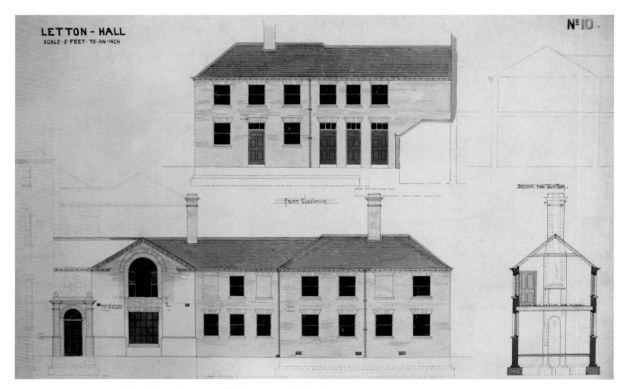

5:4 Elevations of the new Male Servants Wing designed by Edward Boardman, dated 1881.
NORFOLK RECORD OFFICE BR 35/2/67/51

EDWARD BOARDMAN'S WORK FOR RT GURDON

Over the next few decades the firm of Edward Boardman and Son was to be involved in several projects at Letton Hall, but these initiated by RT Gurdon are the first recorded ones.

New Male Servants Wing. (5:4) This scheme provided for an additional three bedrooms on the first floor, with some food storage and preparation rooms on the ground floor; these included a fully-tiled dairy and meat rooms with slate benches. The wing took up the entire north side of the kitchen courtyard, but there is no record of what was there before. Soane had shown some small single storey rooms here in some of his plans for the 'offices', but it is not clear what was eventually constructed. Boardman's wing was well built, in cream coloured brick matching that of the main Hall.

Stable Improvements. Soane's stable block (**3:15** and **3:16**) had remained as planned for 100 years but RT Gurdon initiated a major modernisation (**5:5**), surmounting it eventually with his own initials on the weathervane (**5:6**). A recent architectural survey involving considerable detective work has uncovered some details of what took place at the time.

> 'The ground plan of the stables was maintained, with most of Soane's external walls … but all the ranges were raised by a storey or re-roofed, and the courtyard elevations were largely altered. Boardman's stable block no longer had the low Palladian appearance of Soane's original but rather a slightly French seventeenth century air.
>
> The first part of the work designed in 1881…consisted of re-ordering the side ranges to provide more useful stabling and carriage houses at ground level, raising the South range by a storey to provide staff accommodation and the North side by a half storey for hay lofts. The second phase of the works, drawn a year later in 1882, was to replace Soane's West building with a two-storey building providing further staff facilities, tack room and clock tower…' [33] **(5:7)**

The finished result is most effective, and completes the balanced courtyard-feel of the buildings. It emphasises the symmetrical axial layout that John Soane was so keen to establish, and, although not in his style, could well have been acceptable to him since Soane himself spent a significant part of his career 'improving' his predecessors' buildings.

5:5 The North elevation of the Southern Stable Wing as drawn by Edward Boardman in 1881, modifying Soane's original design.

NORFOLK RECORD OFFICE BR35/2/67/12

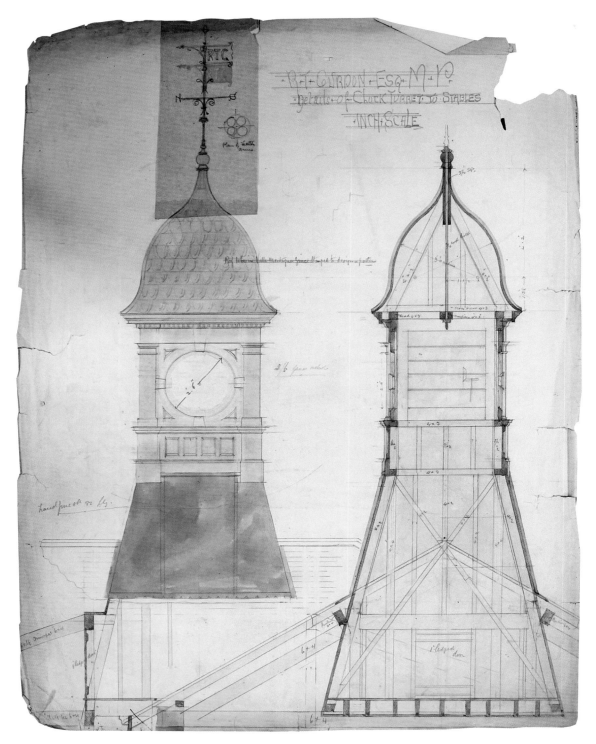

5:6 Boardman's drawing of the clocktower surmounting the central stable block with the initials 'RTG' on the top of the weathervane.

NORFOLK RECORD OFFICE BR 35/2/67/42

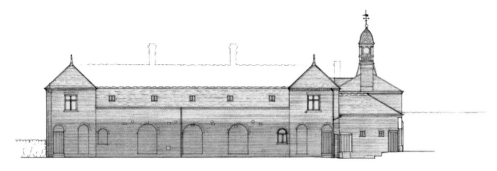

NORTH ELEVATION

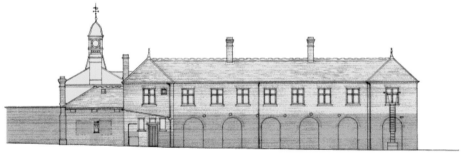

WEST ELEVATION

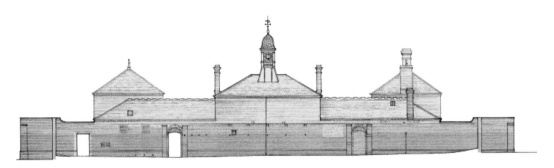

SOUTH ELEVATION

KEY

Soane work of 1786-1789

Existing in 1881 as surveyed by Boardman (some may be as originally built by Soane)

Boardman alterations of 1881-1882

Early 20th century alterations

Late 20th Century alterations

Dating is based on study of surviving original drawings and examination of the existing fabric.

EAST ELEVATION

5:7 Elevations of the stable buildings drawn by Nicholas Jackson, interpreting the changes that have taken place.
REPRODUCED BY COURTESY OF NICHOLAS VANBRUGH LTD

Gardens. Boardman produced a whole series of drawings ranging from general layouts of the grounds, to details of flowerbeds, and to alternative designs for sets of garden steps.

The general layout he proposed seems to have been implemented, including garden walks and an ornamental lake with rustic bentwood bridge over it (see picture in Appendix II, p153). One can imagine many political plans being hatched along the new paths, and all manner of family hopes and ambitions, and friendly confidences, being shared in walks beside the lake. A very useful addition to the Hall's facilities.

Garden steps (**5:8**, **5:9**) were also built which, although rather grand for the modest access they provided, were no doubt useful for all manners of social posing, posturing and general interchanges. A conservatory was also added to the Drawing Room, by Boulton and Paul, 'Horticultural Builders, Norwich' (see picture in Appendix II, p153).

5:8 A sketch by Edward Boardman showing a scheme for a flight of ornamental steps outside the East façade of the main house.
NORFOLK RECORD OFFICE BR 35/2/67/5

5:9 Design for the steps in the Italian Garden, as eventually constructed.
NORFOLK RECORD OFFICE BR 35/2/67/24

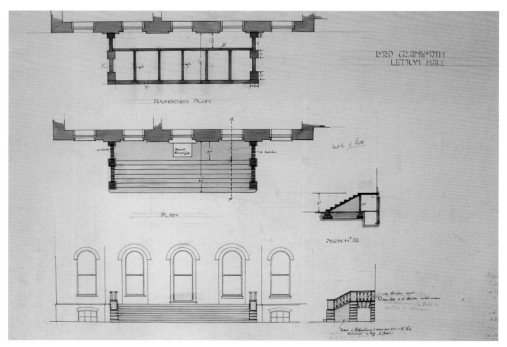

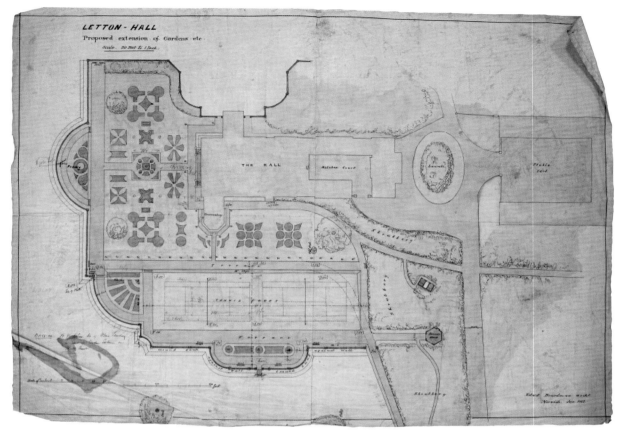

5:10 Boardman's proposal for the layout of the formal gardens, drawn in 1882.
NORFOLK RECORD OFFICE BR 35/2/67/11

Apart from the general layout there is no evidence that the over-fussy ornamental flowerbeds Boardman proposed (**5:10**) were actually installed. Already there were several gardeners employed but these extra beds would have needed at least two or three more men; the flower beds would have added a lot of colour and interest to the garden – but at a substantial cost.

A charming summerhouse was added, once again with practical benefits for constructive leisure use (**5:11**). The style was 'country cottage' with thatched roof and rustic porch – and another example of the not-so-discreet detail in the form of 'RTG 1882', in carved brick, set in the chimney stack.

A pair of garden privies also formed part of this plan, located about 30 yards from the summerhouse in one direction and about 50 yards from the new servants' wing in the other. They were substantially built but rather primitive in function one would have thought, even for this period, particularly as they were located so close to living quarters.

Although not strictly related to Letton Hall itself, it is interesting to note that around this same time, the nearby church of St Andrews Southburgh, within the bounds of the estate, was being rebuilt. The church tower had been burnt down in the eighteenth century, and was being replaced at the same time as other refurbishment. The work was carried out under the direction of the diocesan architect JA Reeve and the cost of nearly £5,000 was paid for largely by the Gurdon family. The Hon. Mrs Henrietta Gurdon, RT Gurdon's mother, died during this time and the slender spire and tower were dedicated to her memory. This church and spire,

5:10 Design by Edward Boardman for a summerhouse to be built in the gardens close to the main house (NORFOLK RECORD OFFICE BR 35/2/67/54) together with a photography of the summerhouse as it exists today.

adjoining Church Farm and set in the midst of gently rolling fields forms, in the author's view, one of the most attractive village church cameos in Norfolk.

Cranworth Church also benefited from the Gurdons' generosity with a new organ in 1888. This was part of a long-standing tradition as the South Porch and Chancel had been rebuilt by the Brampton Gurdons' at a cost of £1,500 in 1852. Also the Cranworth School had been built in 1844 and supported by Theophilus Thornhagh Gurdon.

RT GURDON'S LEGACY

Although there were no more major building projects within RT Gurdon's time the impression left is that he put a lot of himself into Letton; he seems to have left his personal mark on the house and gardens in a more pronounced and enduring way than perhaps any other owner. This was not merely by the obvious device of having his initials displayed in various places, but more by bringing the buildings to a completeness and balance that would not have existed before.

Once brought up to standard by this burst of work, the house served as a backdrop to RT Gurdon's very busy life. *The Times* of 14 October 1902, gives some idea of the pace of his political life.

> 'He was returned by South Norfolk in 1880, and sat for it until 1885, and afterwards for Mid Norfolk from 1885 to 1886, when he was re-elected as a Liberal Unionist. In 1892, he was defeated by Mr Higgins QC a Gladstonian Liberal, who when Mr Higgins accepted the Chiltern Hundreds in April 1895, Mr Gurdon was once more elected, his opponent being Mr Fredrick Wilson. In the following July, however, Mr Wilson defeated Mr Gurdon who did not afterwards enter Parliament.'

Life did not quieten down completely even after RT Gurdon's retirement from the House of Commons, for he served as Deputy Lieutenant of Norfolk, maintained his role as Colonel of the 4th VB Norfolk Regiment and in 1899 became first Chairman of the newly formed Norfolk County Council, a post he held for three years.

In this year came what is seen by many as the high point in his life, when he was created first Baron Cranworth. It has been suggested that this was a 'consolation' peerage after so many set backs in his political career, as if there was somehow a sense of non-fulfilment in his life. However, viewed in perspective, it seems entirely appropriate to see it as a culmination of a long and successful career in public service.

The Times of 14 April 1902 reported the comments of his colleagues in the Norfolk Quarter Sessions who expressed:

> 'their sense of the admirable manner in which for many year he has presided over their deliberations and conducted the business of the Bench. His attention to all matters which came before him, his excellent judgement and conspicuous ability, his great sense of justice and fairness, his patience and unvarying kindness and courtesy not only lightened the burden of his brother magistrates, but made it a pleasure to work with him and endeared him to them personally'.

They wished him a peaceful retirement from public life, secure in the knowledge that his services were much appreciated; but sadly this retirement was not to last long.

On the 13 October 1902, Lord Cranworth died and was buried in St Mary's, the parish church of Letton and Cranworth. The service attracted representatives from his associates, and from all the major families of Norfolk, but was also a simple and homely occasion, The coffin was borne in from the hearse by tenants, and the service which *The Times* described as 'of the simplest character' included the hymn *Now The Labourer's Task Is Over*. A modest end to a rich and varied life.

1   Norfolk Record Office, MC 76/44/1

2   *Armstrong's Norfolk Diary – Further extracts from the Diary of Rev BJ Armstrong*, Hodder and Stoughton 1963. (referred to as Book 2). p31.

3   This extract does not appear in either Book 1 or Book 2 but has been contributed by a correspondent who merely cites "Armstrong's Diaries". There are known to be more volumes published but the author has been unable to locate them.

4   Book 2 p45.

5   Several generations have listed Brooks's as one of the clubs to which members of the Gurdon family belonged.

6   Book 2 p46.

7   *A Norfolk Diary – Passages from the Diary of Rev BJ Armstrong*, George Harrap, 1949 (referred to as Book 1) p30.

8   Book 2 p55.

9   In neither Books 1 or 2 but contributed as (3) above.

10 Book 2 p76.

11 Book 1 p 68.

12 Book 2 p94, but the author's correspondent adds the words '*Our darling Helen*' which are not in the Book 2 version.

13 Book 2 p95.

14 Book 1 p97.

15 Book 1 p105.

16 Book 1 p119.

17 Book 1 p127.

18 Book 1 p145.

19 Book 1 p149.

20 Book 1 p160.

21 Gibbs and Doubleday, *The Complete Peerage*, 1913.

22 Book 1 p162.

23 Book 1 p169.

24 Book 2 p136.

25 Book 1 p232.

26 Book 1 p232.

27 Dr Pam Barnes *Norfolk Landowners since 1880*, Centre of East Anglian Studies, University of East Anglia 1993, p15.

28 Ibid. p15.

29 Ibid. p15 ff.

30 Book 2 p176.

31 See Ref. (27) above, p45.

32 Norfolk Record Office BR 35/2/67. More than 50 drawings and sketches are available, although several are in a fragile condition.

33 Nicholas Jackson, *Architectural History Report – Letton Hall, Dolphin Court*, Nicholas Vanbrugh Limited, 2010. The author holds a copy of this report on file.

EDWARDIAN INTERLUDE

To the casual observer of Letton, nothing seemed to have changed in the general way of life as Edward VII came to the throne, apart from the passing of the first Lord Cranworth. Bertram Francis Gurdon, the 2nd Baron Cranworth succeeded at the much younger age of 25. Nine months after the death of his father, he married Vera Emily, daughter of Mr and Mrs AW Ridley of Eaton Place, London.

The Times of 20 July 1903 reports that the wedding took place at St Peter's Church, Eaton Square, with a reception held afterwards at the residence of the bride's parents, and adds that the bride was attended by a page and fourteen bridesmaids.

A year later Robert Brampton Gurdon was born, as recorded in *The Hingham Deanery Magazine* for September 1904.

> 'On Sunday, August 7th, at a special afternoon service, Lord and Lady Cranworth's little son and heir was baptised by the rector in Cranworth church. The font was beautifully decorated by Mr Watson, head gardener at Letton Hall. The church was crowded with parishioners, and with tenants from neighbouring parishes etc. The lesson was read by Lord Cranworth, a special sermon was preached from St. Mark X:14-16 and specially selected hymns etc. were sung. Lady Cranworth has given a beautiful oak lectern to Cranworth church with the following inscription 'In Thankful Remembrance Of June 21st 1904 RBG''. [1]

The Lady Cranworth referred to as giving the new lectern was probably the fond grandmother, Emily, Lady Cranworth, widow of the first Lord Cranworth. The lectern itself is carved in the form of the figure of an imposing eagle carrying the Bible on its wings.

In its October 1905 issue the *Hingham Magazine* carries another evocative report:

> 'On September 4th, Lord and Lady Cranworth most kindly entertained all the children attending the Day and Sunday school, and also the Reymerston children, at Letton Hall. The weather was all that could be wished, and the children thoroughly enjoyed the games, swings etc, and all the good things provide for them. Lord and Lady Cranworth themselves took part in the games, superintended the races, and did all they could to make their little guests happy. Fire balloons were sent up in the evening and were a great success. The children showed their appreciation by giving hearty cheers for Lord and Lady Cranworth before leaving, and for the Hon. RB Gurdon who waved his acknowledgements from one of the windows.' [2]

But behind those windows there must have been many discussions and conversations taking place about the future. Outwardly, life continued as it had for many years. As the church magazine reports again:

> 'through the kindness of the Cranworths, a Christmas plum pudding was sent to every cottage in the three parishes. Widows, widowers and the aged and infirmed also received Christmas presents from the hall' [3].

6:1 Bertram Francis Gurdon (1877–1964) 2nd Baron Cranworth.

But there were other issues that had to be faced.

It was an 'Indian Summer' as Mark Girouard says in his book *Life In The English Country House*:

> '...exceedingly agreeable, but bound to come to an end. On green lawns or under spreading cedar trees countless tea tables were still being spread with white table cloths, and hostesses still poured out tea from silver tea pots. Nothing, it might seem, had changed. But in fact a great deal had changed'. [4]

The apparently tranquil Edwardian interlude was merely a break between the security of Victoria's reign and the beginnings of the Great War. It was in fact a period of great change and almost a complete reversal of traditional values. These changes were to result, within ten years, in Letton being sold and Lord and Lady Cranworth moving to Grundisburgh Hall in Suffolk. But these decisions were not made lightly or quickly; and as well as national and world-wide considerations there were several local developments still to come at Letton.

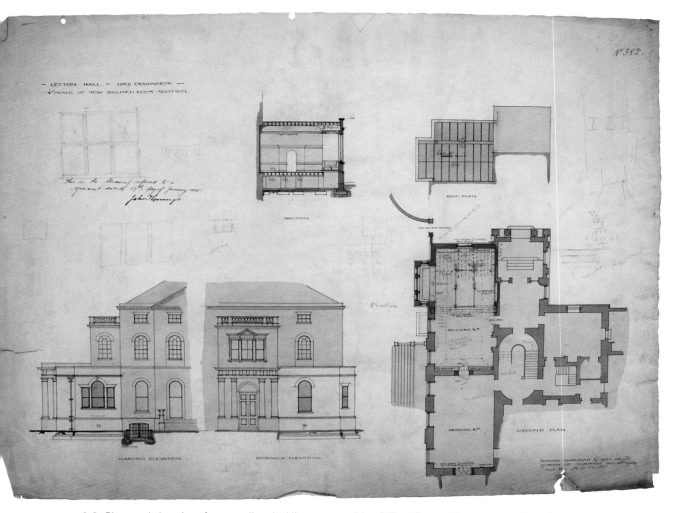

6:2 Plans and elevations for extending the Library to provide a Billiard Room. These were produced by Boardman and Son in 1904, and the work was implemented and exists in this form today.

NORFOLK RECORD OFFICE BR 35/2/67/18

6:3 The Billiard Room, as shown in the Auction Sale Particulars of 1913. (See further particulars in Appendix II)

Edward Boardman and Son, the architects, were called back and ET Boardman and his client embarked on what was to be a most significant project; the extension of Soane's Library at the south-east corner of the house to form a Billiard Room. This work was completed and the extended Library exists more or less exactly according to Boardman's plans (**6:2**).

Opinion varies greatly over the finished room. From the inside, although Soane's symmetry had been destroyed, some of his proportions remain and his original bookcases have been retained. Drawings of these are in Sir John Soane's Museum[5] (**3:6**) and is interesting to see that Boardman in his own drawings refers to them being relocated, .[6] From the inside, the room is attractive and practical; and from the point of view of Letton's present use, where a comfortable conference and meeting room is required, visitors almost invariably vote it 'the best room'.

From the outside it adds nothing good to the elevations; but it can be argued that the real damage to Soane's façade was done when the entrance porch was added, several decades previously, and at least the extension to the Library didn't make that any worse. Whatever the verdict, the new room is a permanent addition. Its use as a Billiard Room is illustrated well in figure (**6:3**) although it has now reverted to being known as the Library.

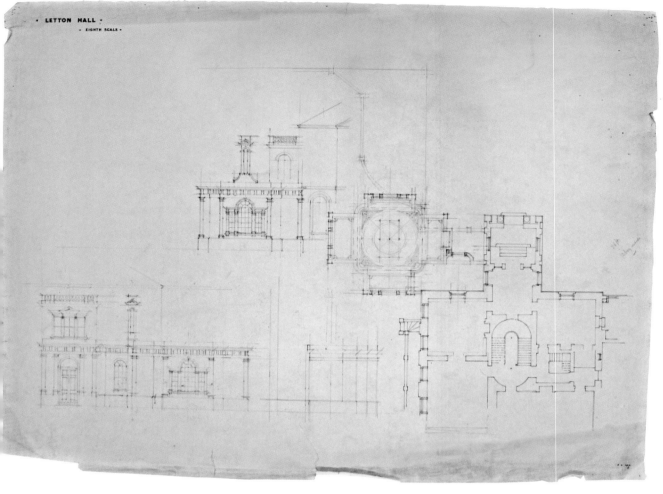

6:4 A sketched scheme by Boardman for a major remodelling of the front elevation of the Hall, produced just a few months before adopting the more modest layout that exists now.

NORFOLK RECORD OFFICE BR 35/2/67/45

What is also fascinating is to speculate on what *might* have been. Within the collection of Boardman drawings in the Norfolk Record Office are several that appear to be imaginative flights of fantasy, whether on the part of the architect or the client isn't clear. Some of them appear to be architectural sketches of alterations or additions that have little obvious purpose or realistic purpose. One (**6:4**) shows the south (entrance) elevation of Letton transformed, as if the architect, recognising that the non-Soane entrance porch sticks out like a sore thumb, has decided that if he can't beat it, he'll feature it; he has extended balustraded terraces and galleries across the façade and then added several other decorative features just to emphasise the point[7].

Another drawing, which is perhaps an alternative to the Billiard Room extension, shows a kind of pavilion alongside the entrance but it is not clear what useful function this would serve. Yet another perspective sketch (**6:5**) shows a most ornate room, possibly the interior of the 'Pavilion'; in a rather interesting way this has echoes of a Soane scheme produced for another building (**6:6**).

6:5 An imaginative perspective sketch by Boardman and Son of the interior of the 'pavilion' that they included in their previous scheme, alongside the front entrance.

NORFOLK RECORD OFFICE BR 35/2/67/32

6:6 John Soane's sketch of a similar 'pavilion' room.

BY COURTESY OF THE TRUSTEES OF SIR JOHN SOANE'S MUSEUM

The Billiard Room was completed, but these other rather fanciful ideas were not implemented. Apart from other considerations these look to be very expensive, almost extravagant, as if their main purpose was to advertise wealth. This prompts some thoughts about the finances of the estate at the time the second Lord Cranworth inherited it.

According to Gibbs and Doubleday the first Lord Cranworth's will was 'proved at £87,000 gross, and £64,000 net' [8]. Although a considerable sum, this was substantially less than the £200,000 quoted for his father 20 years earlier. However, one needs to be very cautious in drawing precise conclusions from figures such as these; Death Duty had now been extended to include agricultural land, and had been swiftly rising, no doubt leading to restructuring of estate finances.[9] Nevertheless, the figures suggest that at least resources were not limitless, and the time might not have been right to be considering elaborate building schemes.

It was a time, however, for increasing links between the land-owning classes and the world of business and industry. There were many seemingly attractive investments to be made, and ways open for estate owners, facing falling agricultural incomes, to make better use of their assets.[10] It is possible that the ambitious building plans may have been in anticipation of lucrative investments that never materialised.

Other commentators have tried to assess the situation by rather more pragmatic means. Dr Susanna Wade Martins indicates that Letton may have been a victim of its own success – or at least a victim of its own policies as a caring landlord and supporter of the community.

> **'The picture gained from the archives is of a small well-run estate commanding good rents throughout the nineteenth century. Estate expenditure was high in the 1880's, presumably in an effort to keep old tenants and to attract new ones in the years of depression, and this is reflected in farm layout…there is every reason to believe, given the good reputation of the estate, that farms were generally kept in good repair. Up to 1887 the estate only paid half the labour costs of repair bills and supplied the materials, but after that the estate met the full cost of repairs. Other expenses were the maintenance of cottages and the estate school, which was entirely financed until 1873'. [11]**

THE GURDONS LEAVE LETTON

Whatever the financial state of the estate, and whatever other considerations came into the picture, the momentous decision was at last made to sell Letton and move to Grundisburgh Hall and to the estate in Suffolk.

The family view now is that the decision to move was probably made for a number of reasons, as these things often are. Even if there was a compelling financial reason, it need not have entailed a move; there were more-or-less equivalent estates in Suffolk which could have been sold with the same result. So there clearly had to be other reasons.

The different people involved would have had differing views. Emily, Lady Cranworth, as a relatively young widow of 52 at the time of her husband's death never made the move to Grundisburgh, and instead stayed at Red House, Southburgh, within sight of the church that had been restored by her family. Perhaps she felt strongly that her late husband had put so much of himself into Letton, and she didn't want to break that emotional tie.

Her son, too, had spent practically all his life at Letton, and may have found the decision to move hard to take; he had however, seen military service in the Boer War and spent additional time in Africa. Did he perhaps foresee more military activity ahead? He did in fact serve with distinction in the 1914–18 war, being awarded the Military Cross and the *Croix de Guerre*.

Another reason for consideration is that the architectural and garden fashions of the day may have had a strong influence. Edward Lutyens was very much the style; he loved generous roofs and bold chimneystacks, houses 'settled into their surroundings'. In his early works, his houses were linked in style to the irregular and sometimes half-timbered Medieval or Tudor manor houses.[12] This was the style of the day, and it was everything that Letton was not.

Likewise, the fashionable garden of the time was in the style of the queen of Edwardian gardeners, Gertrude Jekyll; a naturally rambling cottage-style garden, full of herbaceous borders on the verge of running wild. And the fashionable Edwardian lady was a hands-on gardener, not merely overseeing a team of gardeners committed to formality and order. [13]

Grundisburgh offered all that Lutyens and Jekyll were promoting, and it is quite easy to see how personal preferences, perhaps of Lady Cranworth especially, were enough to swing the decision to leave Letton.

It must have been an enormous decision to sever the links with a house and estate that had been established over so many generations, and one can only speculate at the discussion and debate that took place. But the results of decision are starkly laid out in the Particulars of Sale, extracts of which appear in Appendix II.

1   Several copies of *The Hingham Deanery Magazine* are in the possession of Mr and Mrs Edward Jackson of Southburgh, to whom thanks are due for these extracts. Copies of the relevant pages are held by the author.

2   Ibid.

3   Ibid.

4   Mark Girouard, *Life in the English Country House*, Yale University Press, 1978. p300.

5   Soane Museum Vol. 57/22, showing ceiling and bookcase details.

6   Norfolk Record Office BR 35/2/67/18. He refers to *'Old bookcases from the Drawing Room'*, but from the context and from the drawings themselves it is clear that it is the Library to which he refers.

7   Norfolk Record Office BR 35/2/67…?

8   Gibbs and Doubleday, *The Complete Peerage*, 1913.

9   Pam Barnes, *Norfolk Landowners since 1880*, Centre of East Anglian Studies, University of East Anglia, 1993. p55 ff.

10   See ref. (4) above, p300 ff.

11   Dr Susanna Wade-Martins, *Historic Farm Buildings – including a Norfolk Survey*, Batsford, 1991. p101–5.

12   See ref. (4) above, p307.

13   Ibid. p314.

THE BACHELOR HOUSEHOLD
OF MR ARTHUR GORDON

In the property market, 1913 was not a good year for country estates; but it marks the next phase of Letton's life. Knight Frank and Rutley, the auctioneers and estate agents, were commissioned to handle the sale and *The Estates Gazette* reported that 'Howard Frank conducted sales with great panache. He was a popular auctioneer from London and a regular at sales in Norfolk. At the auction of Lord Cranworth's 4,498-acre Letton Hall estate in 1913, the opening bid was a mere £40,000. With good humour, Mr Frank thanked the gentleman for his offer, but made it clear that he did not consider it a realistic bid. Even when put up in separate lots, the main lot failed to find a bidder, and consequently the greater part of the estate was withdrawn'. [1]

So it wasn't until 6 July 1914 that Arthur Wiener Gordon (**7:1**) purchased Letton, ending 130 years of the Gurdons' ownership of the Sir John Soane house, and several hundred years of them being principal land owners in the area. Of the family, only Emily, Lady Cranworth now remained, aged 64, and she was to live in Red House, Southburgh for another 20 years.

Arthur Gordon was a bachelor of 37, living in Sussex Square, Hyde Park, London at the time, a director of Johnasson and Gordon Ltd., shipping and colliery owners, and of other companies. He had been born in Sunderland County Durham in July 1877 son of Frederick Gordon, then of the Briery, Sunderland but of Scottish descent. He had been educated at Charterhouse School, and at Trinity College, Cambridge. Frederick had died in 1905, and Arthur, 28 at the time, had taken over the running of the business.

On the 28 June 1914, just a week before Arthur Gordon bought Letton, the Archduke Francis Ferdinand, heir to the Austrian throne, was shot dead in Sarajevo by a Bosnian fanatic, an event which brought about the declaration of war by Great Britain some six weeks later. In the midst of this stormy time, Letton changed hands and began the next phase of its life. Whatever short term predictions the experts made at the time, the Great War was to last four years and changed ways of life in all the countries involved, even in rural Norfolk.

Arthur Gordon spent the war years working in the Admiralty in London, where his shipping experience – and probably his ships too – would have been extremely useful.

Not much is recorded of life at Letton during those years. Presumably Mr Gordon, the new Lord of the Manor, was obliged with his other preoccupations to leave the estate to run itself for a while – but Letton didn't escape involvement completely.

The story is told of an incident early in the war when a detachment of artillery were camped on the front park with their horses. One night there was a violent storm, and the horses broke loose and bolted into the surrounding fields and farms. The following morning search parties were sent out but only a few horse were ever found… who knows what barns or stables in the neighbourhood were a little fuller after that night! There's no official record of this incident

7:1 Arthur Wiener Gordon (1877–1965)

anywhere, just the story told with a Norfolk knowing look [2]…nothing seems to have been put in writing by anyone, but then that is hardly surprising.

Further research raises the possibility this could have been part of a requisitioning exercise carried out under the Defence-of-the-Realm Act. In 1914 during the early years of the war, officers drove around the countryside by car, collecting whatever horses they felt were needed, drafting in apparently 165,000 horses from the country as a whole.[3] There was a procedure for horses to be returned in case of hardship, but all the same, one can imagine the reaction of many Norfolk farmers to this; no wonder they took advantage of the storm.

After the Armistice of November 1918, Arthur Gordon began to put his own stamp on Letton. A complete set of beautifully drawn plans (**7:2**) of the Main Hall and Servants Wings are at Letton, prepared by Hampton and Sons Ltd., Builders and Engineers of Pall Mall, London, and dated February 1919. There are no structural or layout changes proposed and the main work done at this time was to the services, in particular lighting, central heating, and water supplies.

The engine-driven electricity generating unit was installed at this time, replacing the Petrol-Air Gas system [4] referred to in the auction particulars of 1913.[5] The electrical control and fuse board still exists in Letton's cellars. (**7:3**)

An interesting insight into the operation of this system is given in a letter dated 17 June 1920, sent from London and signed by Mr Gordon, addressed to Mr Disdle, 'Electrician, Letton Hall…' In it Mr Gurdon explains he has ordered an initial delivery of 300 gallons of oil, with the same quantity every two months after that. (**7:4**)

There was also extensive work carried out on the water supply system at this time. A spring appears on the Ordnance Survey maps even going back to the earliest editions, at Newell's Head, some half a mile or so from the Hall (see Appendix II, p152). In addition to wells within the immediate curtillage of the buildings (for instance in the NE corner of Soane's laundry room) this had been the main source of water for the property for many years, and is certainly recorded as such in 1913. However, no mention is made of how the water is transferred from the spring to the Hall.

There are the remains of a 3-cylinder reciprocating pump driven by a water wheel in the Spring House, and there is also a single cylinder Lister Diesel operating another reciprocating pump. But Mr Gordon must have felt that these were not adequate for he also installed a pair of Blakes Hydrams. During work on the system in 1996, the manufacturers were able to say that these were first supplied on the 11 September 1919, to the order of a Mr Gordon – and moreover, they still had some spares on the shelf. Impressive after-sales service.

The hydraulic ram principle is worthy of note. It relies first of all on a continuous supply of running water; in Letton's case, this is provided by the spring bubbling up into an enclosed spring pool some 20 feet across and up to six feet deep. This is allowed to flow quickly down a six-inch diameter pipe to the ram. The flow is then stopped suddenly and the energy of the

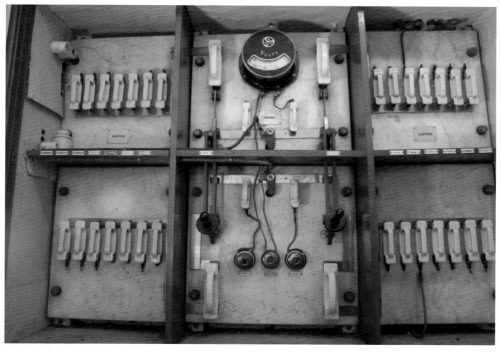

7:3 The electricity distribution panel sending the 210V DC supply to various locations from, for instance, the Boudoir to the Female Servants Wing, with a special feed to the Heating Motors.

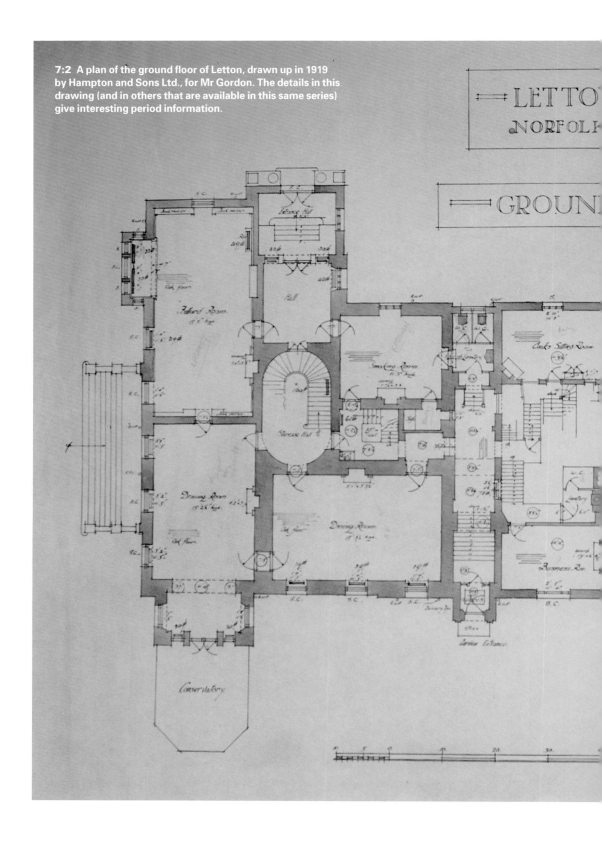

7:2 A plan of the ground floor of Letton, drawn up in 1919 by Hampton and Sons Ltd., for Mr Gordon. The details in this drawing (and in others that are available in this same series) give interesting period information.

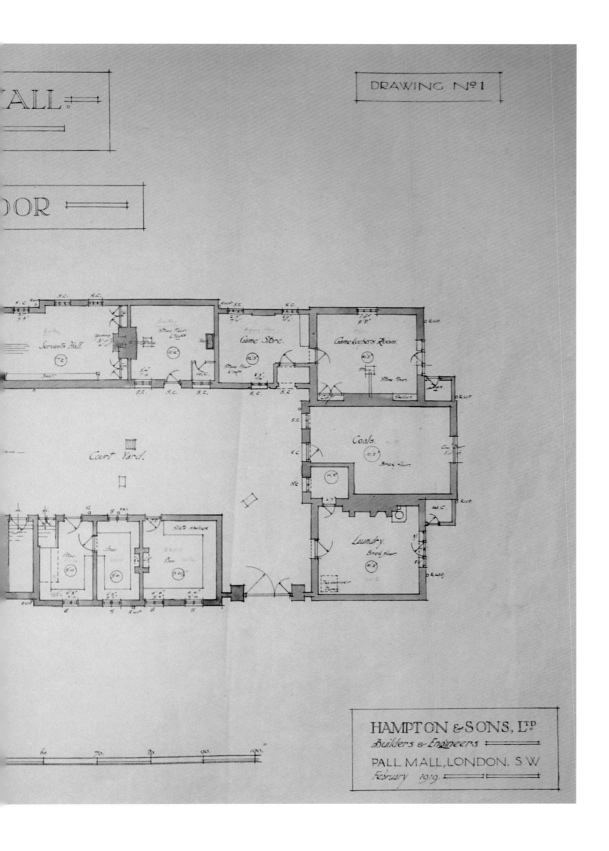

DRAWING Nº 1

HAMPTON & SONS, Lᵀᴰ
Builders & Engineers
PALL MALL, LONDON. SW
February 1919.

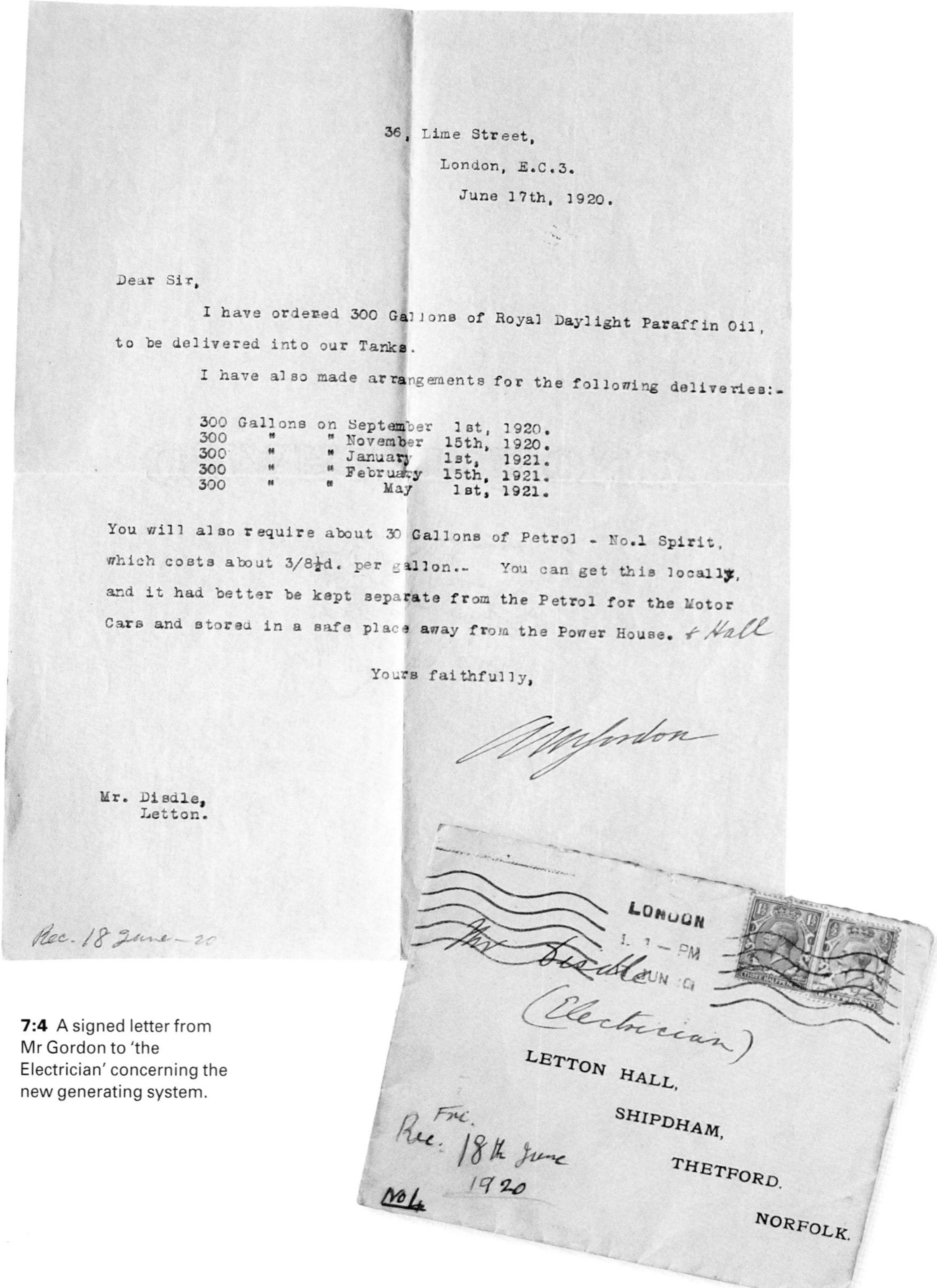

36, Lime Street,

London, E.C.3.

June 17th, 1920.

Dear Sir,

I have ordered 300 Gallons of Royal Daylight Paraffin Oil, to be delivered into our Tanks.

I have also made arrangements for the following deliveries:-

300 Gallons on September 1st, 1920.
300   "   " November 15th, 1920.
300   "   " January 1st, 1921.
300   "   " February 15th, 1921.
300   "   " May   1st, 1921.

You will also require about 30 Gallons of Petrol - No.1 Spirit, which costs about 3/8½d. per gallon.- You can get this locally, and it had better be kept separate from the Petrol for the Motor Cars and stored in a safe place away from the Power House. + Hall

Yours faithfully,

Mr. Disdle,
Letton.

Rec. 18 June - 20

7:4 A signed letter from Mr Gordon to 'the Electrician' concerning the new generating system.

94

fast-flowing water 'rams' a small quantity of water at surprisingly high pressure to its point of use. In Letton's case this is half a mile away and 150 feet higher. The thump-thump of the rams, operating continuously around the clock, provides an eerie 'heart beat' in the woods round the spring.

All these improvements were set to support the new life of Letton, and it seemed as if it was going to be a busy life. Mr Gordon was away in London and abroad for considerable periods, but despite only being at Letton for a few months each year, he arranged shooting parties regularly. As a racing man with horses stabled at Newmarket he entertained his friends and associates back at Letton. He also welcomed the West Norfolk Hunt for meets, and it is rumoured that on one occasion the Prince of Wales (later to be King Edward VIII) was present. All these activities endorse the impression in peoples' minds of an era of glamorous occasions.

After the Great War, Arthur Gordon gradually withdrew from his shipping interests, and made other investments. However, he still maintained his overseas connections, particularly with Germany. He was also able to pursue a life-long involvement with racing, and owned racehorses with trainers at Newmarket; and he devoted a great deal of time to overseeing his agricultural estate, building up the Cranlet herd, as described later.

BELOW STAIRS IN THE 1930s

Dealing with the more recent aspects of Letton Hall's history brings the advantage that events are now within the living memory of a number of people. Thus stories have a more personal note, with a freshness and sense of immediacy that rarely comes from official records. People are happy to recall in an informal chat much more than they would ever consider writing down in a formal way; and of course the source of anecdotes has often been the Servants' Hall.

In 1986 an energetic lady, proudly acknowledging more than 70 years of age, walked up Letton's drive from the village of Shipdham. *Walked* mind you, when even the most athletically-aspiring young person of today would demand a bike, if not a car, for the same journey.

She had been in service at Letton from her late teens until she married in her early 20s. Her name was actually Miss Letton at the time, but is now Mrs Boyd. [6] She started as second housemaid, and rose to be head housemaid by the time she left, having celebrated her 21st birthday at Letton in 1934. She told enthralling stories of how, for instance, she used to arrange to visit the toilet in the Female Servants Wing at a specific time each day, so she could court Rix, the baker's boy, through the first-floor window at the end of the corridor, as he made his deliveries.

She shared her room with Nora Ram, a fellow housemaid, and one night they had stayed too long at a dance in the village. To return to their room the official way meant creeping past the door of Mrs Britton, the dragon housekeeper – and there was a glass panel in this door, so placed in the narrow corridor that it was impossible to duck below it. Worse than that, once past, they had to scuttle the full length of 'Baker Street' (the nickname given to the long straight corridor of the Female Servants Wing), in full view of anyone who cared to look out before they could reach the sanctuary of their own room. They decided against the risk and instead roused a couple of stable boys from their loft rooms over the horses a hundred yards away and persuaded them to set up a ladder so they could climb in through their bedroom window. Apparently they managed it successfully and lived to tell the tale.

Life 'in service' had quite a buzz about it, and with Mr Gordon often away in London or overseas, the true 'life at Letton' centred round the kitchen courtyard rather than the Hall Drawing Room; all the younger members of the staff had racing bikes and were known in Shipdham as the 'Letton Gospels'.

The 'indoors' or hall staff were generally remembered as 'about nine or ten', supplemented by ladies coming in from Cranworth or the other villages, to do the rough cleaning. The list set out below is as remembered by Miss Letton, and is borne out by directories and the recollections of others – but it is very much just a 'snapshot' at a point in time of a household that was always changing.

Butler	Clifford
Footman	Edward (Clifford's brother)
Oddjobman	Cop'hole Jack (referring to his task of lighting the fire under the coppers)
Housekeeper	Mrs Britton
Head housemaid	Miss Letton
First housemaid	Nora Ram
Second housemaid	?
Cook	?
Kitchen maid	Joyce Taylor
Scullery maid	Gladys

It is interesting to compare this number with the 20 or so employed 40 years previously (**7:5**) – although exact comparisons are difficult because of the different categories of servants. Also, the status of any particular house was indicated by the number of male servants rather than the total number.

Reg Gowan [7] was in charge of the pleasure gardens from 1935–39, and as this included the flowers and plants in the hall he had frequent contact with the indoor staff. He remembers Clifford the butler as something of a gambling man who 'when he had a win, had a whet…' He would use the window of his pantry to leave and return undetected – but it wasn't unknown

7:5 A photograph from the files of a local historian showing some of the staff at Letton at a date guessed to be around 1896.

for him to need the help of the footman (his brother), and sometimes Reg as well, to get upstairs if he'd over-indulged. The cook was 'a lovely old lady', and the general atmosphere of the household was happy – 'we had more laughs in a day than most places did in a year'.

Joyce Taylor [8] worked in the kitchens and her daughter has contributed some extracts from her autograph book.

> I guess you've heard of Letton Hall
> A place were maids don't stay at all.
> They call the girls sheep
> The men they call rams
> Don't you believe it
> We're all like lambs
> > *Signed* '**One who knows**'

> A House without a roof my friend
> A ship without a sail.
> But the most uncomfortable thing I know
> Is a shirt without a tail.
> > *Signed* '**EMJ 10.1.1938 Letton Hall**'

> Read   See   that   me
> Up   will   I   love
> And   You   Love   you
> Down   And   You   and
> > *Signed* '**HE 0.1.38**'

> Many a sailor has been wrecked
> on a permanent wave.
> > *Signed* '**N Vas 30th May 1937**'

> There is a place in Norfolk
> The devil knows it well,
> He visits it quite frequently
> And calls it Letton Hell.
> > *Signed* '**HEP 10.1.38**'

But of course the indoor Hall staff were only part of the overall household. There were other specialist roles.

THE CHAUFFEUR

After the house servants, the closest outside servant to the family, was the chauffeur. Up until 1937, Mr Gordon's chauffeur was Mr Sydney Parsons [9], who lived with his family in a flat above the motor houses, along one side of the stable courtyard.

The role of chauffeur was a key one during this time of transition between horses and cars. The Gurdons were definitely horse and carriage people, linking in with the LNER railway stations at Thuxton and Yaxham. But Mr Gordon, although a horse-racing man and using horses on the farms was definitely 'a car man' when it came to personal transport, although he too would use the railway for many trips. 'When a new car came out', it was said by the staff, 'he had one' – generally two or three in the fleet at any one time. As the photographs show there was at least one Rolls Royce and two Mercedes Benz around at this time plus an Austin Seven with van body for general estate work. (**7:6, 7:7, 7:8, 7:10**)

The battle for 'the best car in the world' was well under way, and in the mid 30s Mercedes introduced a magnificent Straight Eight in an all-out attempt to defeat Rolls Royce. Mr Gordon bought one and Syd Parsons drove him to a race meeting in Newmarket, only to have it

7:6 This is one of Mr Gordon's early cars – a Rolls Royce 20/25 of the 1920s.

7:7 Chauffeur Sydney Parsons was also very proud of the Rolls…

develop severe wheel wobble on the journey back. Even when brought to an emergency stop, the whole car continued to tremble like a jelly. 'Parsons', said Mr Gordon, 'This goes back to the Mercedes people in London straight away tomorrow'. It did, and apparently, as others had suffered the same problem, the whole model was withdrawn. To patriotic Parsons this was probably a just ending; he had been put through the Rolls Royce Chauffeur School by Mr Gordon, and it must have been well-nigh-impossible for him not to be partisan.

In those developing days, when the arrival of *any* car at the Hall would have cause a stir, and an actual ride-in–a–car was still a novelty for most, motoring incidents seem to have stuck in people's minds.

Mr Fred Risebro ran the village garage in Shipdham and used a Wolseley saloon – the police car type – as a local taxi. On one occasion he was bringing a new maid to her post and arrived at the same time as bluff Doctor Edwards, the ex-naval GP who was visiting in his old blue Rolls with dickey seat. Dr Edwards came charging out, in a hurry as usual, and leapt into the taxi. Mr Risebro stepped forward and touching his cap respectfully said 'Excuse me sir, I think you're in the wrong car'. 'Damn it Risebro, so I am'. This little incident which stuck in the mind of the nine-year-old patient, Eric, the chauffeur's son, seems to capture the novelty of those early motoring days.

The chauffeur's role at Letton extended to anything mechanical. Sydney Parsons was also responsible for operating the large oil engine, generating DC electricity at 210 volts in the Power House; Eric Parsons remembers the *whoosh-whoosh* as it ran, and the fact that the men on the estate used to bring in their accumulators (batteries) for his father to charge up. Eric also remembers being carried on his father's shoulders through the woods to the hydraulic rams, which were another 'mechanical device' and therefore the domain of the 'man that knew about these things'.

7:8 The estate had an Austin Seven with a van body as a general run-about – and here Eric Parsons, the chauffeur's son, is learning the trade from an early age.

7:9 Mr Gordon outside the front door of the hall looking rather proud – but the car is unidentified.

7:10 This is one of the Mercedes cars that Mr Gordon owned.

Mr Gordon's staff seem to have had nothing but respect for him, and regarded him as a fair, generous and considerate employer. But in March 1937 Syd Parsons was asked to leave; there were no bad relations, no complaints about poor performance, just a policy-change it seems – but the date is very significant. Mr Bill Davies was the next chauffeur, and his arrival was linked with a particularly significant event.

1   Pam Barnes *Norfolk Landowners since 1880*, Centre of East Anglian Studies, University of East Anglia, 1993, p 66.

2   This story was first told to the author by George Hunt, who for nearly 50 years lived in the lodge at the corner of the Front Park.

3   Neil R Storey *Norfolk at war – Britain in old Photographs*, Alan Sutton Publishing Ltd. A photograph in this book shows approximately 20 horses and 15 wagons assembled in Dereham Market Place, requisitioned for military service.

4   Brian Bowers *Lengthening the Day* Oxford University Press 1998. p138 ff gives an account of the 'Petrol-Air Gas System' used in large houses.

5   See Appendix II.

6   Mrs Boyd, of Monkton, Ramsgate. Her reminiscences are held on file by the author.

7   Reg Gowan's recollections of both the indoor and the estate staff are held on file by the author.

8   Mrs Kathleen Adcock of Norwich supplied these details, which are held on file by the author.

9   Mr Parsons' son Eric has contributed a wealth of stories and pictures concerning the chauffeur's role. These are held on file by the author.

MR AND MRS GORDON

By the mid thirties, Mr Gordon had owned Letton for more than 20 years, and was living a settled and fulfilling life keenly pursuing his racing and farming interests; approaching 60 years of age and unmarried, he seemed to be a confirmed bachelor.

But suddenly there was a lady in his life, and not just an ordinary lady but an elegant French lady, half his age – soon to become Mrs Gordon. How the household, indeed the whole estate, must have buzzed and talked and speculated, and watched with fascinated expectation.

8:1 An elegant young French lady makes her appearance at Letton – and here she poses on what appears to be Edward Boardman's bentwood bridge, near the site of the old hall. (See picture, Appendix II, p153.)

In 1998 Mrs Gordon was living near Marseilles and was able to share personally the fascinating memories of her life at Letton.[1]

Mademoiselle Marie Josephine Webber was born in 1905 in Bas-Rhin near Strasbourg in Alsace, the daughter of Joseph Webber whose family had been landowners in that part of France for many years. In the mid 30s she was engaged to be married but her fiancé was dying of polio, and Mlle Webber was spending some time in Paris. There, at a private reception, she met Arthur Wiener Gordon. 'No', she said, when asked whether it was love at first sight and a whirlwind romance, 'but he was kind and attentive and generous – and knew how to treat a lady'. One wonders, even though it may not have been love at first sight for Mrs Gordon, what impact this attractive and intelligent young lady must have had on her future husband; he certainly seems to have been strongly smitten.

8:2 Mr and Mrs Arthur Gordon dressed for a special occasion.

8:3 An elegant Mrs Gordon stepping out of her Mercedes

She visited Letton before they were married and Eric Parsons remembers them walking arm in arm, around the gardens, she very much the elegant and chic French lady. (**8:1**) They were married on 2 February 1937 in Paris, in the Cardinals' private chapel, because she was a Catholic and her husband a Protestant. They were destined for a long and very happy married life together.[2] 'A *very* happy life', said Mrs Gordon, with a nostalgic smile. She said of her Letton days 'it was a time and place I particularly appreciated'.

Their honeymoon had to wait for a year, but was a worthy one when it took place – a three-month world cruise on the *Empress of Scotland*, embarking at Monaco in February 1938. They travelled from England to Monte Carlo aboard the Blue Train with all the appropriate baggage for a long sea voyage; Mr Gordon's toilet requisites alone filled a leather suitcase, fully fitted with all the crystal and silver items necessary for a comfortable trip.

The *Empress of Scotland* was an appropriate choice because Mr Gordon always regarded himself as a Scot rather than an Englishman. This settled one local Letton rumour, which suggested that because of his middle name of Wiener, he had a German background. This idea hugely amused Mrs Gordon; 'He was Scottish, my dear, not a trace of anything else' – and went on to explain that Wiener was the name of an old friend of the family and business associate living in Hamburg.

In Mrs Gordon's room at Marseilles, there were three pictures taking pride of place; one of Arthur and Marie Gordon in formal poses (**8:1** and **8:2**) and one of a dashing young lady in elegant clothes getting out of a Mercedes Cabriolet (**8:3**); someone with an obvious flair for enjoying life to the full. It was Mrs Gordon's favourite pictures herself, taken at a gymkhana in Sussex, and it says a lot about this lady of great personality and presence.

CHANGES IN THE DOMESTIC HOUSEHOLD

However, before her honeymoon, Mrs Gordon had to return to Letton in her new role as mistress of the household; and after the household had had more than 20 years of bachelor rule this needed considerable courage and determination. Arthur Gordon had wisely decided that it was inappropriate to retain those of the domestic staff who had been particularly involved in running the bachelor household, so the daunting and rather overbearing house-keeper, Mrs Britton, left along with others. Mrs Gordon appointed her own housekeeper, Harriet, for a year until the honeymoon cruise. After that she felt she had acquired sufficient experience herself to require one no longer.

A new chauffeur arrived, Mr Bill Davies, with his family including daughters Simone and Paulette. Bill's first wife had been French and he spoke French himself, which may have proved useful at times. Mr Bell the gardener, on the other hand, once insisted in giving Mrs Gordon all the Latin names of the fruits and flowers as he toured the walled garden with her, perhaps feeling that any foreign language was as good as another. From Mrs Gordon's point of view, she says she found the broad Norfolk accents of some of the estate workers completely unintelligible.

Her arrival caused a stir in many ways, and had its amusing moments. Mrs Linda Davies, the chauffeur's wife, who did some private washing for Mrs Gordon, declared herself amazed at the amount of luxurious underwear that a French lady of style seemed to regard as essential. Mrs Gordon had also arranged for a bidet to be installed in her bathroom, possibly the first one in the entire county of Norfolk. The workmen involved in its installation, and those other members of the household in the know, took great delight in sneaking their friends upstairs when the Gordons were not at home, to show off this amazing continental device.

It is interesting to know how the Gordons occupied the first floor of the Hall for their private rooms:

> Their bedroom was the room at the SE corner (now 'Oxford' and 'Ely')
> Mr Gordon's dressing room was over the entrance (now 'Peterborough')
> Their bathroom was at the centre of the E elevation (now 'Exeter')
> Mrs Gordon's dressing room was at the NE corner
> (now 'Cambridge' and 'Guildford')

In looking back over her life at Letton Mrs Gordon said 'I feel I did so little – no great deeds written up in official histories' yet she presided over the details of daily life with style and great success. Her charm and intelligence seemed to have won over everyone, including Beryl, the Davies' young daughter who remembers her as 'one of the best'.

THE GAMEKEEPER

Although the indoor staff had experienced a major change when Mrs Gordon arrived, others more remote from the domestic life of the hall were able to continue their lives with very little interruption.

Mr Wilfred Richardson (**8:5**) – or Wilfred James Darby Richardson, to give him his full name – had been Mr Gordon's gamekeeper since around 1930[3] and lived with his family in the Lodge at the end of the Cranworth drive (**8:6**). Mr Syd Banham, a son of the farm bailiff, was one of three under-gamekeepers and lived at nearby Booters Hall[4] with his family (**8:7, 9:8**).

Wilfred Richardson had the reputation of being a good gamekeeper. One of his tactics was to hang lanterns on poles in the woods on winter nights, so that as they swung to and fro in the wind poachers would believe that they were being carried by someone, and be warned off. Wilf's nickname was 'Skidly'; the reason or meaning isn't absolutely clear but may have been to do with his custom of having hobnails on his boots so that he could slide around in them on hard surfaces.

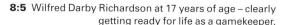

8:5 Wilfred Darby Richardson at 17 years of age – clearly getting ready for life as a gamekeeper.

8:6 The Gamekeeper's Lodge, at the Cranworth end of the Letton Hall drive.

8:7 Booters Hall, situated about half-a-mile south of Letton Hall.

However, some fascinating memories have been passed down about his family including those of his very pretty daughter Girlie, nicknamed 'Goldilocks' because of her golden hair. She used to sing and dance at the Cranworth school parties, and was regarded as the Shirley Temple of the district. She had a younger sister Jean, also very pretty, who broke the hearts of the next age group down. In 1983 Jean's daughter, Janine Frary wrote an account of a Christmas in the 1930s at the Lodge, the Richardsons' family home, for the magazine *Norfolk Fair*.

8:8 Mr and Mrs Harry Banham.

'WHEN A SECOND-HAND TOY MEANT WONDER AND JOY.

The Letton Hall Lodge was surrounded by woodland. My mother, then a small child, remembers listening at night when all was quiet to the owls hooting in the trees. A candle would flicker beside the bed and her toes were warmed by a stone hot water bottle.

At Christmas the Lodge must have been especially cosy. Much preparation was spent to make it thus. My grandmother began baking cakes and puddings in October. The puddings were put into cloths and boiled in the brick copper, normally used for the weekly wash.

A brace of pheasants from the pre-Christmas shoot was given to each family of estate workers. The estate workers were a close community indeed. Without television, and one and a half miles to the nearest village, they provided their own festivity and entertainment.

A party was given by Squire Gordon, for all the children of the village. My mother, aunt and uncle were painstakingly 'got ready' for this event by first washing well in the tin bath. My grandmother must have hated heating the water in kettles, yet to do so was plainly accepted, since running hot water belonged only in the homes of the rich. The girls' hair was put into 'dodmans' before going to bed. On the following morning, the day of the party, all three were dressed in clean pink pinafores, well starched, with huge stiff bows at the sides beneath the arms.

Music for the party was provided in the simplest forms; singing, or sometimes playing the 'comb and paper'. The wireless was only ever used for the news or important issues, being run by an accumulator, and the community were not privileged in having a piano for social functions.

It is strange to compare the difference between the gifts brought by Father Christmas today, and those of 1930. We see, in the 1980s (a mere space of 50 years) computerised games and expensive toys, all packaged superbly. The children of 1930 received a few sweets and some fruit, and one toy, often second-hand. Handmade presents were obviously popular, for example, nightdress cases and hanky sachets.

The children of the past savoured no less the happiness of Christmas because of their spartan stocking. The enchantment came from goodwill and unity, and the smallest rewards – perhaps the candles lit for the first time upon the Christmas tree or finding a threepenny bit in the Christmas pudding.

We have need to be envious of their simple pleasure but I cannot help reflecting also on the amount of hard work every person was obliged to contribute. It is wise to spare a thought for my grandmother, whose toil was made hard having to black lead and white brimstone the kitchen range, scrub the grate, kitchen table and pantry shelves with soda, and spend washday with a bar of soap in place of a washing machine. But I fancy her reward was no less either – especially at Christmas time.' [5]

The Richardsons were to leave Letton and their life in the Lodge in 1940 at a time when there was so much other change in the air; but Wilfred was to take with him the evidence of another painful memory before then.

In 1938 he was out on the estate with his two dogs and as he jumped over a ditch one of the dogs landed next to him and hit the trigger of his gun. The shot caught Wilf's left hand and blasted off his index and middle fingers. He was driven mad with the pain, rushing round the Lodge unable to stop until physically restrained; meanwhile Girlie had to run up to the Hall to call Mr Davies the chauffeur so that help could be brought. Eventually the doctor arrived with an injection, and arranged treatment, after which the Cranworth nurse Mrs Dobbs attended him.

THE AGRICULTURAL ESTATE

The continually developing life and activity of Home Farm and the five or six other farms forming the Letton Estate is a story in itself, and in a sense outside the scope of this book. Much has been researched about Norfolk farms and estates already [6], but it seems worth recording some of the names who are remembered as part of the life of the hall, even though this list is incomplete.

Mr Harry Banham was Farm Bailiff (**8:8**). He lived in Booters Hall and seems to be have been universally liked and respected. He had his roots in this part of Norfolk and several of his family lived or worked on the estate as well. Mrs Gordon remembered him as 'a nice man' even though she couldn't always understand what he was saying, because of his accent.

His grandson, Roy, remembers occasional rides with him as he visited the farms each day by pony and trap, to oversee the work of the men. He also remembers him regularly catching the

8:9 Mr Charlie Banham.

train from Yaxham station to attend Norwich market, buying and selling cattle and sheep for the estate. He generally wore breeches and 'buskins' (leather gaiters): and Roy remembers that he was very keen on time keeping and so kept two watches, one in each waistcoat pocket. One of them was silver, with a pretty face, and Roy remembers his grandfather saying 'When you get your first job at 14 you can have this watch'. He was as good as his word, and gave the watch, which Roy still has. Another thing he gave was vital advice to help his grandson be prepared for anything in life. 'Always carry', he said, 'a shut knife, a shilling and a piece of string'.

Mr George Stanley Joslin was the estate secretary and agent, and lived at Home Farm. He had been appointed before 1925, so was a long-standing employee of Mr Gordon.

Each farm had its foreman, and names that are known[7] include Barnard Briggs at Church Farm, Mr Myhill and Charles Brimm at Gurdon Farm, Isaac Carter at Low Farm and Mr Charlie Banham (**8:9**) at Gurdon Farm. Charlie was one of the first to fill the role of what would now be called agricultural engineering. He worked as mechanic and tractor driver and it was said that all he needed to get any machine on the farm working was a piece of string.

Messrs Kenny Graves, Rivett, Williamson and Pidd were general farm workers. Mr Tuttle was the shepherd, and there were a number of other specialists remembered including Mr Fawkes, the blacksmith from Shipdham and Mr Tuddenham the maintenance worker who lived in Park Cottages.

It is interesting to note that despite Arthur Gordon's enthusiasm for cars as personal transport, he was a keen breeder of Suffolk horses on the farm estate. Frank Graves and Jack Juby were both horsemen and lived on Blackmoor Row near to where the horses were stabled at Gurdon Farm. Jack was head team-man by the time he was 21 and remembers the Gordons as 'the sort of people you showed respect to…you touched your hat to them, and it was a pleasure and honour to work there'. He added 'I would like to have another 10 years like that'.

These were eventful years at Letton but clearly other changes were afoot in the life of the estate; in October 1940 Mr Gordon offered Booters Hall Farm and its stock for sale by auction. Whatever his reasons for selling, the auction particulars[8] give a picture of the size and activities of part of the estate at that time.

Booters Hall –
497 acres with farmhouse and 9 cottages
Stock – 20 Suffolk horses and 86 head of pedigree Angus cattle
(including the pedigree Suffolk mares Letton Bessie,
Letton Prima, Letton Shiner and Letton Secunda)

The records state that most of the cattle had been bred by AW Gordon Esquire, and say that the land 'has been farmed in hand by the owner'.

Further sales took place in 1944 of 11 more Suffolks and 'the well-known Cranlet Red Poll Herd of approximately 140 head' from Home Farm and Gurdon Farm.

THE GARDENS

Like the agricultural estate, the gardens had a life- and work-cycle of their own that went on regardless of the happenings in the Hall; as long, that is, as there were financial resources available. Unlike the farm, the gardens had no easy means of paying their way, and their justification had to be made in terms of leisure and pleasure, and of continuing and conserving what had been created in the past. The kitchen gardens would of course have made a contribution, but this was more in terms of 'feeding the hands that tended them' rather than in a significant net gain.

Happily in the time of Mr Gordon, resources *were* available. In the time of later occupants, the gardens were to come under increasing pressure, but in Arthur Gordon's time they were kept impeccably as some of the contemporary pictures show. (**8:10** and **8:11**) The clipped shrubs, and crisply edged lawns and pathways, with weeded beds and well stocked glasshouses would have given that instant impact of a well-ordered estate, owned by someone of substantial means. Many people remember Mr Gordon's time as the heyday of life on this large estate.

Despite the fact that Edward Boardman Senior's ambitious plans of 1880 had not been fully implemented, the gardens still required quite a sizeable team to maintain them. Opinions vary over exactly how many gardeners there were, although 'around six' seems to be the general consensus – but it's difficult to escape the picture of green clad stalwarts toiling away from dawn to dusk in distant corners, anonymous, uncounted, but always there.

As well as the mystery over how many gardeners were employed, the post of Head Gardener also raises some anomalies:

Kelly's directories for 1925–33 list John Meachen as 'Head Gardener to AWG – but Eric Parsons, a contemporary, said it was Horace Meachen.

Kelly's directory for 1937 lists H.W. Bell as 'Head Gardener to AWG' – but Reg Gowan who as Head Groundsman, worked for him from 1935–39, said it was John Bell.

It is also remembered that Jock Bell (not to be confused with John Bell), an itinerant Scot came as second gardener but only stayed for three years as he said 'He never stayed at any employment, anywhere, longer than that'.

To confuse the issue still further the Davies family said that Mr Marsh, 'the gardener' in 1937, lived at Gardeners' Cottage (**8:12**) – the domain of the head gardener.

One can question the reliability of memories, but when such close working and living relationships are concerned, it seems surprising; no doubt there is a solution although it is now lost in time.

This uncertainty over how many gardeners there were, and over their names, seems to confirm the notion that the gardens themselves were an accepted backdrop to the Hall. Their existence and well-kept availability for leisured strolls was taken for granted as part of the life of the Letton Hall estate. They were part of the changeless country house scene that seemed as if it would go on for ever.

But major change was just around the corner as the shadow of World War II spread as far as Norfolk.

8:10 'The Kennel Garden' is to the south of the Servants' Wing.

8:11 These were some of the glasshouses within the walled garden, along the south-facing wall.

8:12 Garden Cottage, the domain of the Head Gardener.

1   Mrs Gordon spent several hours over a period of three days with the author, sharing her memories and giving her views on people and events. This material, including a video recording of interviews and a copy of all the relevant personal photographs, is retained on file by the author. It is not individually referenced in the main text.

2   *The Times* of 7 October 1965 reported the death of Arthur Wiener Gordon, aged 88, of Petworth, Sussex, former racehorse owner. He left £440,618 and a donation of £200 to St Dunstans.

3   Mr Richardson appears as 'Gamekeeper to AWG' in the Kelly's Directories for 1933 and 1937.

4   Booters Hall had been part of the Letton estate for many years and is described in the 1914 Particulars of Sale (see Appendix II). It was situated approximately half-a-mile SE of Letton Hall, and was used as accommodation for various of the Estate staff. It was destroyed by fire around the 1960s.

5   *Norfolk Fair – The County Magazine*, December 1983, p44.

6   See in particular Ref [1] in the previous chapter, and also Dr Wade Martin's *Historic Farm Buildings* Batsford 1991.
    Dr Wade Martins with Alan Carter also produced *A Year in the Field*, Centre of East Anglian Studies, University of East Anglia 1987, which includes information on the Letton Estate.

7   The names listed in this chapter for the Estate workers come from a variety of sources including Kelly's Directories of 1916, 1925, 1929, 1933 and 1937 and anecdotal evidence from, in particular, Mr Roy Banham. Details are held on file by the author.

8   Sale Particulars in the Norfolk Record Office, BR 143/29 and /184–8.

WORLD WAR II

There are some momentous announcements that once lived through are never forgotten. The time, the place, the little details of where and when they are first heard are imprinted on the memory.

At 11.15 am on Sunday, 3 September 1939, when Mr Chamberlain announced over the wireless that Britain was at war with Germany, Roy Banham[1] remembers standing with some members of his family by the iron gates at Booters Hall, where he was living with his grandparents, Mr and Mrs Harry Banham. He was only seven at the time, unable to understand fully what was happening, but the gravity of it all was borne out by the reactions of everyone around him; serious faces, questions without answers, excitement mixed with fear.

It was obviously not a complete surprise, because talk of war, building of air-raid shelters, practice blackouts, exercises and all sorts of unfamiliar activities had been going on for months. But now that it had actually happened it was something of an anti-climax; no one was really sure what to do next or what to expect.

Many things of course came into official being at that point: black-out, strict response to air-raid sirens, the carrying of gas-masks at all times, temporary closing of some schools, shops and offices, the curtailing of regional services of the BBC etc., – but nevertheless life went on without dramatic change. It seemed wrong somehow, now that Britain was officially at war; as far as rural Norfolk was concerned, it was only the 'phoney war' that had started.

On the Norfolk coast it was very different however, because war at sea started much more decisively. On 3 September ships were sailing the high seas freely about their normal business when suddenly they were vulnerable to U-boats. By 9 pm that night the passenger liner *Athenia* had been torpedoed and lost. Around the coast of East Anglia enemy patrols could be seen, and the sights and sounds of battle gave war a reality.

But in the countryside, with seemingly little change from peacetime, the sudden imposition of all kinds of restrictions must have seemed unnecessarily irksome and the product of over-zealous officialdom. When the air-raid sirens go, and once again there is no air-raid, quite soon the sirens lose credibility. In writing about what he called this *twilight war* from September 1939 to May 1940, Winston Churchill quotes from letters to Neville Chamberlain, still at that time (October 1938) Prime Minister. He says it should be recognised that different parts of the country were exposed to different degrees of danger.

> 'London of course is the chief target…[but] **over the great part of the country-side modified lighting should be at once allowed, and places of entertainment opened…In these areas, which comprise at least seven eighths of the United Kingdom gas masks should be kept at home, and only carried in the target areas as scheduled…'**[2]

It appears that in these months before hostilities reached inland Norfolk, the precautions themselves sometimes did more damage than the enemy. Road accidents increased enormously in the first few months of the black-out, while the number of people sporting black-eyes, and chipped noses elbows and knees became astronomically high.[3]

Schools reopened after their short-term closure and Roy Banham remembers cycling there one day and getting his gas mask caught in the front wheel. He came off and broke his arm – but remained stoically at school, in the spirit of wartime, until told he should go home.

Mr and Mrs Gordon stayed living at the hall until the outbreak of war, but then moved to the Red House at Southburgh which Arthur Gordon had bought on the death of Emily, Lady Cranworth in 1934. Edward Boardman and Son, the architects, had been called in and produced a number of drawings of extensions and improvements between 1935 and 1938[4], but whether even then Arthur Gordon was intending to live there himself at some point isn't clear. At any rate, the house was available and the Gordons moved in.

They had offered the main hall to the Government for use as a convalescent home, but this offer was not taken up. The house and stables were, however, requisitioned a little later in 1940,[5] as were so many properties throughout East Anglia; and sometimes, it seems, properties were 'taken over', even without the formality of requisitioning.[6]

Mrs Gordon recalled those days, but when asked whether she felt any resentment or even anger at having to leave the house to which she had arrived in such style only a few years said 'No, we had to do what ever had to be done. It was war-time.' She remembers other changes too such as having to use bicycles to get around. They still had the cars of course but without much petrol available these spent most of their time in the garages. Mrs Gordon, in common with all the other wives on the estate, turned her hands to whatever she could do to help the war effort. She remembers it as a very busy time for her: doing such things as running First Aid courses and coping with much less help in the house.

But this is jumping ahead a little. What Churchill called *this strange autumn and winter*[7] had given the British Expeditionary Force a breathing space to set up in France; and to help the French and Belgians in setting up their defences, albeit as a very tiny proportion of the total numbers of troops involved. Mrs Gordon remembered it as a very worrying time for her, as she thought of her family in Alsace. After the early days of war there was no reliable way of keeping in touch; as the battles raged in France, was her family safe? Were they still alive? The country had been invaded and overrun by Hitler in a way that had seemed unthinkable before 1939.

As the German army invaded more of Europe with an aggressiveness which rapidly destroyed resistance it became clear that this was going to be total war, and its impact would reach rural Norfolk very quickly.

By 4 June 1940 the famous Dunkirk Flotilla had done its work, and nearly 350,000 British and Allied troops were back in England – although all their vital equipment and weapons had, of necessity, been left behind. The shock waves and aftermath of this critical event were felt far and wide, and certainly reached Norfolk.

A contingent of battle-weary soldiers came to the newly-established base at Letton to recuperate, and to regain strength for the next phase. The French were still fighting on although with little strength left, and Britain was pledged to continuing the battle to destroy Hitler completely.

Having seen how quickly and ruthlessly the German Army had over-run Holland and Belgium, and broken through to invade France, the threat of invasion of Britain now had to be taken with the utmost seriousness. East Anglia was seen by many as one of the most likely and vulnerable areas for this invasion to take place. A revised strategy was devised, following the recent experiences and worked on with great urgency.

The establishment of the Home Guard was a key element in this counter-invasion programme. It never had a chance to show its mettle because an invasion was staved off by other means, and it has suffered ever since, perhaps unjustifiably, from not being taken seriously. But it took very seriously its task of preparing to defend the home front, despite minimal equipment and the competing priorities of war (**9:1**).

9:1 The Cranworth contingent of the Home Guard, including several members of the Letton Hall Estate.

There was now a severe shortage of weapons, equipment, transport and supplies, partly due to what had had to be abandoned in Dunkirk, and partly due to the rapid growth of the Army itself. Also there was a need to provide at least the basics for the Home Guard.

One of the units of the army whose task it was to meet these needs was the Royal Army Service Corps, and it seems that for most of its military life Letton was an RASC base.

MILITARY RECORDS

At this point it is relevant to comment on the availability or otherwise of official records covering the activities of places such as Letton during the war years. So little has been found that one is led to suspect either that whatever happened at Letton was either so top-secret that all records have been destroyed, or else so mundane that no one thought it worth recording.

For several English counties full records exist of all requisitioned properties in so-called *Blue Books*, but regrettably no *Blue Book* exists for Norfolk. Presumably this information was destroyed after the war, except for properties where there was major war damage or claims outstanding. A formal request to the Ministry of Defence was met with the answer that 'We regret that we cannot find any information on this property'.[8]

There was some evidence that the Canadian Army were based at Letton for some part of the war, in the form of Canadian information sheets still posted on the wall afterwards; and also, more lively evidence, in the shape of a black Labrador puppy left with the Banham boys, when its Canadian Army owner was posted overseas. But when an approach was made to the Director of History, National Defence Headquarters, Ottawa, the reply was, 'It is regretted that we are unable to assist you, owing to the prohibitively lengthy research that it would necessitate'.[9]

The most fruitful source of information and leads in this detective trail has proved to be personal visits by people who were themselves stationed at Letton.

Driver J Northwood left a note saying he was stationed at 'Letton Hall HQ' from 1940 to 1941 and was attached to '46th Division Eastern Command'. It appears he was part of a 'Ammunition Company', which gave some clue as to the work which was done here.

Driver FE Plane visited to see again the place at which he was stationed in early 1944. He left a note to say that he was with 310 Company, RASC. The fact that he was another driver confirmed the general impression held by local people that whatever the Army did at Letton it was to do with transport.

There were often lorries dispersed along the lanes all along the neighbourhood, parked under trees or under camouflaged netting, to minimise the risk of air attack. Again the memory of the young Roy Banham comes into play, as he remembers once being diverted on his way back home from school, because of a lorry on fire at the corner of Blackmoor Row. It had been a very hot day, and the lorry was one of three parked in a copse beside the road and had caught fire. Because it was an ammunition lorry it caused rather more than a routine emergency. Nearby soldiers had to push the other two lorries out of range before it all developed into a major incident.

Mrs Ivy Adland also revisited the scene of some of her wartime memories and wrote it all down.

> 'I was stationed at Letton Hall from May to December 1942 in charge of the NAAFI canteen. At first I thought I had been deported to the wilds of nowhere! However, I came to find a great love for the beauty of the district and particularly of the Hall and grounds. The unit stationed at the estate was the 25th Tank Brigade Company, RASC, consisting of three officers and around two hundred men. The officer and the senior NCOs were billeted in the Hall and the other ranks in Nissen huts near the stables, which were used as workshops, company stores etc. I was sent with three other girls to take over from the male personnel, and our canteen was the room at the right of the main door. One of the men was an excellent pianist and entertained us quite often on the NAAFI piano. The unit also had a dance band and many pleasant evening were spent at village halls and other camps.
>
> The room at the left of the main door was the CO's office and the room leading off it was the Officers' Dining Room. At the top of the main stairs the room on the left was the Company Office and the room next to it was the officers' and senior NCO's Mess, to which we were often invited. My office was a small room along the corridor on the first floor with the adjoining room as a bed-sitting room.
>
> I cannot remember any concert parties ever coming to entertain us. We did however put on our own concerts in Shipdham village hall, to which the villagers were invited. We enjoyed the produce of the gardens and greenhouses for which I thanked the gardener weekly.
>
> We became like one large family. We even had a Christmas cake made – but orders were received that the Unit was moving to Claydon in Suffolk and as there were no more troops coming in, we would also be moved. We moved out on 23rd December with great regret. I look back in those months as some of the happiest of my life.'[10]

Ivy also remembered a couple of names, Sergeant James Pemblett of Northwich, Cheshire and a Lieutenant Wheelwright, and added 'not much to go on I'm afraid'.

But what she provided was the vital code with which to break into the vast store of information in The National Archives in Kew. Cross-referencing '25th Tank Brigade' with 'RASC' and '1942' produced a slim file marked *SECRET – WAR DIARIES*[11] (**9:2, 9:3, 9:4**). What great secrets did it contain? – but it turned out not to be nearly as dramatic as it sounded.

For instance, the Company Commanding Officer, Major J Hay Morgan, recorded for all the 31 days of October 1942 'No Entries' – but then the work itself was probably not very dramatic. Typical jobs might have included repair and maintenance of military vehicles, filling of Jerricans to form mobile fuel stores, packing and loading of ammunition boxes and transport to wherever needed. Also there would have been driver and mechanic training in order to be able to maintain supplies to whatever unit they were servicing. On the face of it, seemingly

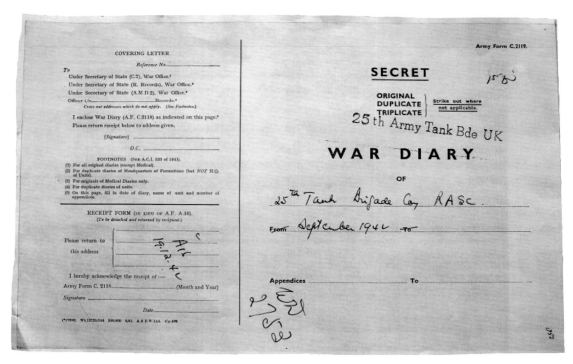

9:2 The cover page of the Secret War Diary for the RASC unit billeted at Letton.
THE NATIONAL ARCHIVES NO 166/9408

mundane work, but so vital to success on the battlefield. Another page of the War Diary (**9:4**), whilst not for Letton itself was in the same file and for an RASC company supporting the same Brigade, so it seems reasonable that the work and pattern of life were similar.

There is a certain 'ordinariness' about the pages, with entertainment organised, community events and an All Ranks dance arranged. But the grim reminders of the war are always there in the background. The troop viewed captured film of German invasions, in areas where no doubt other members of RASC would have served and possibly given their lives.

The RASC served with honour and distinction in all theatres of the war. It provided some awesome statistics: operating more than a million vehicles, providing millions of ration packs, procuring millions of reusable cans for petrol etc. It also provided countless stories of tasks which, although seemingly humble, were nevertheless vital in the urgencies of war. This is one:

> '…during the Dunkirk evacuation, the duty officer of ST3 received an urgent phone call from a worried patrol officer at Dover, to the effect that the troops on the beaches of Dunkirk were in desperate need of drinking water. The ST3 officer thought and acted quickly. Within a few hours, two MT Companies were loaded with sixty thousand of the new cans, held at Slough, and were on their way to Dover. At the coast they were filled with water and shipped to the Dunkirk beaches in time to save the situation'. [12]

Perhaps the best way to round off this record of the RASC at Letton is the words of the Divisional Commander of the 51st division, on 12 June 1940 at St. Valery. They had fought gallantly, and held on to their position longer than expected but with terrible losses, with their supply lines cut off and their evacuation back to England no longer possible. After the capture of the Division, which included the RASC Unit supplying them, he addressed his commanders, and gave this tribute, 'The RASC never let us down' [13].

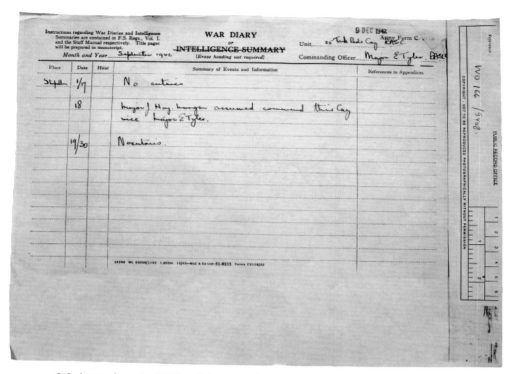

9:3 A page from the RASC unit diary – as plans were being made to move out of Letton.

THE NATIONAL ARCHIVES NO 166/9408

9:4 A further page from the 25th Army Tank Brigade RASC diary, and although this was not at Letton the work and pattern of life would have been similar.

THE NATIONAL ARCHIVES NO 166/9408

THE AMERICANS ARRIVE

When the first construction crews arrived in 1941 to build an airfield at Shipdham, part of it within Letton estate land, it would have been impossible to imagine in advance the enormous impact this would have on the neighbourhood (**9:5**). The airfield was to provide accommodation for 460 officers and 2,660 enlisted men; storage for more than 200,000 gallons of fuel and hard-standing area for 50 aircraft. Construction could be said to have made an explosive start, since the trees throughout the site were literally blown out of the ground.

In an *Eastern Daily Press* article in 1993 Pat Mallett said there were sad memories of the home where he grew up demolished overnight to make way for Shipdham airfield. 'They just took it, we had no choice' he said. 'They didn't give you compensation or anything in those days'.[14]

Shipdham was the first heavy bomber base in Norfolk and was continuous host to B24 Liberators for longer than any other Eighth Air Force combat airfield in Britain, from October 1942 to June 1945. The 44th Bomber group became known as '*The Flying Eight Balls*' because its personnel felt they were always left until last – like the black ball in a game of pool.

They flew a total of 343 missions, with its gunners credited with 330 enemy fighters shot down. Its own losses however were heavy, amounting to 153 aircraft – an average of one per week over the entire operational time.

But it was the people not the statistics that made the made the main impact on the Letton estate and the surrounding villages. With the bomb dump less than half a mile from the Hall, and the nearest estate cottages virtually on the perimeter of the airfield, there was obviously going to be a lot of 'neighbourly contact', particularly with such outgoing people as the Americans.

The young boys of the area made early contact. Roy Banham remembers hearing the first aircraft arrive. Before long he and his brothers and friends were on sweets and chewing-gum terms, graduating soon to ride in Jeeps, and eventually enjoying more or less complete freedom of the perimeter road. As a matter of course they counted the aircraft out and in again, doing the grim arithmetic. This side of war made an impression on them when once, just before Christmas, the school was invited to sing carols to the injured airmen in the base hospital. They were driven out there in one of Mr Walter Rudling's buses, blacked-out since it was after dark, and stood in the middle of a large Nissen hut to sing their pieces. As well as some terrible injuries, there were also hands bandaged and faces blackened with frostbite, through flying high in cold weather. The war was made very real to the children when they saw it could hurt people this badly.

On a more mundane level, the US Air force men needed their clothes washed. No doubt there were facilities on the base for doing this, but one suspects that having it done outside gave an opportunity to share in a little family life, perhaps even to be mothered a little. Certainly several families on the Letton estate helped out and earned real and lasting gratitude for it. Linda Davies, wife of Bill Davies, the Gordons' chauffeur, helped out and over 50 years later was still attending reunions of visiting American veterans on the airfield. 'You may not realise it', one of them told her in 1992, 'but you saved my life by looking after me'. A great reward from such a small service, and the grateful airman had remembered it for a long time.

May Banham, Roy's mother, also used to do washing and the men would drop it off at her cottage on Blackmoor Row. Her sons noticed the difference when aircrew occasionally called in straight from a mission, wanting clean clothes to change into. Most of the flyers were cheerful and easy-going – but after a mission they were withdrawn and tense, dirt-grimed and sweaty. Sometimes a man never did call in to collect his washing, and it was a poignant and painful task to return the washing to base for parcelling up with all his other personal possessions.

(6-8008)(12-3-43) SHIPDHAM AIRDROME

9:5 An aerial photograph of Shipdham airfield, with Letton Hall just visible in the top left hand corner. The cottages of some of the estate workers were even closer than the Hall.

PHOTOGRAPH BY COURTESY OF 44TH BGVA

There were good times too of course. Parties on the base, and regular patronage of *The Royal Standard* and other pubs in Shipdham. Bicycles were dug out of sheds in the village and loaned to the airmen. At one point the Base Commander complained good-humouredly that it would all have to stop because he was having more casualties from falling off bikes than from all the flying missions put together.

Ensuring law and order seemed to be good humoured too, generally, and although there were the military police to call on if necessary, a lot seemed to be sorted out 'at local level'. The Shipdham village constable was PC Wilkins, who was assisted by Roy's father Charlie as a Special. On one occasion an airman from the base had taken to hiding in a roadside copse of trees and appearing whenever he saw a woman approaching. When Roy returned home from school that day his mother told him to go straight into the village and tell PC Wilkins that his father had gone into the woods after the airman. As Roy returned, he saw his father sitting on a bank beside the road, with his twelve-bore across his knees and the 'prisoner' sitting beside him, apparently quietly waiting to be dealt with.

RAF FLYING ACTIVITIES

Living close to an operational airfield obviously led to a lot of airborne excitement. As well as the coming and goings of the American Liberators based there, Shipdham was used by other aircraft either returning home damaged or short of fuel, and the Hall itself was said to be used as a plotting point by RAF Pathfinder Bomber Pilots.[15]

Graham Smith in his book on Norfolk Airfields gives an account of a dramatic RAF incident:

> 'On the night on 3rd November 1943 the Americans at Shipdham played welcome hosts to a most distinguished pilot and his crew. A heavily damaged Lancaster of 61 Squadron based at Syderstone near Newark was staggering back from a raid on Dusseldorf, when the pilot, Flight Lieutenant William Reid spotted some searchlights. Reid, who was suffering severe injuries, knew that the aircraft would not make it back to base so he circled the airfield and flashed his landing lights as a warning to the ground crews of his damaged aircraft. The effort involved in circling the aircraft had resulted in reopening Reid's serious head wounds, which greatly impaired his vision. Nevertheless he still managed to bring the Lancaster down onto the runway but immediately the undercarriage collapsed. The aircraft carried along for about fifty yards before finally coming to a halt. One of the crew was already dead and one died later in the Shipdham medical centre. Reid was later awarded the Victoria Cross for this raid on Dusseldorf and the citation read '…tenacity and devotion to duty beyond praise'. He later joined 617, the Dam Buster Squadron, and was shot down in July 1944 but survived as a prisoner of war.'[16] **(9:6)**

Roy Banham remembers the visit of another Lancaster, with a less fortunate outcome. About four or five o'clock one wintry afternoon, his father Charlie was sitting with his back to the window reading a newspaper, when he noticed the paper glowing red in his hands. He looked out of the window and a blazing plane was coming down on the field across the road. Two parachutes were also coming down within three or four hundred yards of the cottage, and he rushed out to go over to them. One was fine but the other needed a stretcher. They told him that the plane still had a 1,000 lb bomb on board. By now the Americans had arrived at the blazing aircraft to try to put out the fire – so Charlie rushed over to warn them to keep well clear. They left the plane to burn, but the expected explosion never came. A guard was put on the area until the bomb could be disposed of and the bodies of the remaining crewmembers removed as far as possible. The next day the Army Bomb Disposal unit arrived, only to find the bomb some 50 yards away. Had it been released early through some mechanical failure,

9:6 A picture of the Lancaster bomber that crash-landed at Shipdham on the night of 3 November 1943. It was piloted by Flt. Lt. Bill Reid, who was subsequently awarded the Victoria Cross.

PHOTOGRAPH BY COURTESY OF 44TH BGVA

moments before the crash? Or had a still-surviving crewmember released it to avoid an explosion on impact? If there had been a crewmember still alive in the burning plane should they have tried to put the fire out? These were some of the many unanswered questions of wartime.

In April 1942 there was a campaign of regular bombing of Norwich and being only fifteen miles away as the bomber flies, there were regular air-raid warnings in the Letton area. May Banham had taken a dislike to sleeping in their air raid shelter because of the toads which slept there too. They had developed the routine of sleeping in the kitchen – May and Charlie on one side of the range and the boys on the other. That night an enemy bomber decided to drop a 'landmine' in the area. These were actually naval mines and were of a far larger tonnage than had been carried in aircraft before. They were released by parachutes from a height of up to 5,000 feet. Because of the complete inaccuracy of this method, it was obvious that the Germans at this time were not concerned at all about whether they hit civilian targets. Soldiers who watched it come down at about 5 am said it narrowly missed the cottages and exploded in the field near Rawbrig Lane.

Inside the cottage the explosion sounded terrible. The windows held because they were shuttered up from outside but the greenhouse was destroyed and the pantry door blown in. Charlie crawled across the kitchen to see if the boys were okay and threw himself on top of them to protect them from further blasts. They were fine – although rather squashed – and after an interval when everything seemed to have gone quiet, May said she would light the oil lamp. When she did this, and they looked at each other, they had the biggest shock of all; soot had been blasted down the chimney, and completely blackened all their faces apart from eyes and teeth.

The closing stages of the war moved on, with most of the action overseas. But the role of those serving on the home front, even at Letton, was not forgotten. In January 1944, General Montgomery was appointed Commander of the Allied Ground Forces for Operations Overlord, and set off on a tour of bases in preparation for D-day. He visited Letton and his visit is still remembered – but only the occasion and not the words or to whom he addressed them.

What would he have made of it, as the end was in sight? As in so many other places there had been drama and excitement, VCs earned and lives lost, within the orbit of the estate. There had also been the humdrum work of military backup and support; there had been amusing incidents and entertaining moments – and there had been pain and suffering and heartbreak. Even in the heart of rural Norfolk, Letton had experienced its share of the triumph and tragedy of war.

When it dawned, 8 May 1945 was a day of celebration and joy, but Churchill's words in November 1942 could well apply to the peace that was about to be worked out at Letton: *This is not the end. It is not even the beginning of the end. But it is perhaps, the end of the beginning.* [17]

1   The author is greatly indebted to Mr Roy Banham for his many recollections referred to in this chapter. They are not individually referenced in the text. Details are retained in the author's files.

2   WS Churchill *The Second World War – Volume I – The Gathering Storm* p384

3   Derek E Johnson, *East Anglia at War*, Jarrolds, 1978, p11

4   Norfolk Record Office, BR 35/2/67/5 to /14.

5   References for 'Requisitions' for Letton have been supplied as Norf/1003, /1243, /2746 and /4524. These have not been consulted.

6   As an instance of this General Robert Broke told the author of an incident in early 1940. He had returned home on leave to stay with his mother at Holme Hale Hall and was awakened early in the morning by military sounds not only in the grounds but also inside the hall itself. His mother confirmed that the army was in the habit of using the tree belt around the house for exercises and, yes, had taken to using rooms inside the house as well. This seemed something of a liberty to Robert Broke, even for wartime, so he sent for the officer in charge of the party; and even in pyjamas and dressing-gown the military bearing and authority of Robert Broke (then a Lieutenant Colonel) soon restored order.

7   WS Churchill – as above, p370.

8   In a letter to the author, from the Ministry of Defence ref. D/Lands/17/4 15 April 1980.

9   In a letter to the author from the National Defence Headquarters, Ottawa 16 May 1980.

10 Mrs Adland, writing as Katie Adland, has collected her memoirs in a book entitled *A Shy Girl's War*, published privately in 2001. The author holds a copy in his files.

11 Public Record Office/ The National Archive ref. WO 166/9408

12 *The Story of the Royal Army Service Corps 1939–45* Published by the Institution of the RASC, 1955, p433.

13 Ibid. p83.

14 *Eastern Daily Press*, Friday 5 November 1993

15 This information was contributed by Mr Richard Milton-Worssell from personal connections within the Air Ministry.

16 Graham Smith, *Norfolk Airfields in the Second World War*, p220. A fuller account of this incident appeared in the *Eastern Daily Press*, 4 November 1993.

17 WS Churchill, made during a speech at The Lord Mayor's Lunch at the mansion House, 10 November 1942.

A FAMILY HOUSE
FOR THE EGLINGTONS

During the war people had faced up to all sorts of unfamiliar and taxing situations and had coped well, showing great courage. Now the war was over a new kind of courage was needed in picking up the pieces and in getting things back to 'normal'. But some of the 'pieces' were widely scattered and broken, and it often wasn't easy.

The main staircase at Letton is the focus of the house and is an architectural masterpiece; thirty steps finely carved from large slabs of Portland Stone are set into the walls to create a seemingly unsupported structure of breath-catching engineering and fascinating aesthetics. A delicate curving balustrade is supported by slender cast iron uprights of an intriguing but simple design. For most of its life, using it was the preserve of the privileged; during the war it was apparently for officers only, with other ranks relegated to the back stairs. After the war it was different.

Several heavy, cast-iron coal-burning stoves had been installed by the Army in the first floor rooms and once the house was de-requisitioned, these had to be moved out. A rear guard of two or three men had the task, and proceeded to drag the stoves down the stairs.

CRASH CRASH – at each step a chunk of Portland Stone was broken off the nosing of the stair.

CRASH SCRAPE CRASH – the stone was softer than the iron and scratched deeply as the stoves were dragged down.

BANG CRASH CRASH – you couldn't really blame the rear guard. They *were* the rear guard because they couldn't keep up with the advance party. The military priority was to progress forward, and more men couldn't be spared.

CRASH CRASH – anyway no one was watching or supervising, it wasn't that important. Except one young girl was watching – someone whose task later, with her family, was to bring back the house to be once more a well –loved home. Picking up the pieces was going to be painful.

CRASH CRASH – round the curved stairs, each one so finely made to match precisely its partner. The stoves took the easy way down, cutting the corner, dragging heavily against the banister and balustrade.

CREAK CRASH – as the handrail flexed and bent, and more stone broke away from where the iron balustrades were set in.

CRASH CRASH – couldn't they use planks? Or pulleys? Or the other stairs? Nothing in the orders about that. Did it matter? Did anyone care that much?

CRASH CRASH – shortly after the war Arthur and Marie Gordon returned to look at the Hall. 'Should we come back and live here?' asked Mr Gordon 'For ten thousand pounds we could have it'. But he couldn't come back. 'He loved that house' said Mrs Gordon. 'It would have broken his heart'.

10:1 An illustration from Pevsner's *Buildings of England* of Letton's main staircase, clearly showing damage left after World War II.

REPRODUCED BY PERMISSION OF ENGLISH HERITAGE NMR

CRASH CRASH – each stair took its punishment, one or two or more large chunks taken out. Leaving it jagged, gappy, like a toothless crone.

CRASH CRASH – some things can never be restored, once destroyed. Sir John Soane's Museum in London has a staircase like Letton's – but a smaller less imposing and impressive version. They have had to repair a few steps – but the repair shows. It's not like new and in any case it cost £1,000 a stair.

CRASH CRASH – nearly at the bottom. Only one or two stairs escaped the damage.

CRASH SCRAPE CRASH – if a house can be said to have a soul, surely this would have felt like the agonies of death. Could it ever recover from this assault and abuse at its heart? Many houses didn't. The late 40s and early 50s are black decades in our architectural history.[1] Was it the end?

CRASH CRASH – it was nearly the end of the job. One more stove and then a NAAFI break, and the end of the detail. The old HQ unit could be left for the civvies to have…

An exaggerated account? The evidence of the damage is there; several people have remembered the circumstances that caused it. Nikolaus Pevsner photographed the staircase (**10:1**) and includes it in his reference work[2] opposite pictures of Sandringham House – which has the effect of emphasising the staircase's poor condition. The damage has only been superficially repaired, sufficient to allow the painful sight to be concealed by carpet.

The incident serves to highlight the attitudes that existed, perhaps of necessity, during- and immediately post-war; sometimes irreversible changes occurred over these years. The break from residential ownership, with its careful oversight of affairs, was something from which many houses never recovered.

The process of taking the house back and attempting to save it was critical and needed real determination.

THE EGLINGTONS TAKE OVER

During the early years of the war Arthur Gordon had transferred ownership of Letton to a property-holding company, the Bradford Property Trust. On 9 September 1944 this Trust offered the Letton Hall estate for sale by auction through Messrs Bidwell and Sons.[3] By now, after sales of various other farms and parcels of land, it amounted to 957 acres including the Hall, seven farms or smallholdings, and several cottages. Including the Hall itself, there were now 27 dwellings.

Mr Samuel George Eglington – known as George to distinguish him from his father Mr SS Eglington – had been farming all his life in various parts of Norfolk, including Foxley, Bawdeswell, Salhouse, Costessey and Weston. His father had encouraged him to try out new ideas, and he had already achieved some success with Welsh pigs and a development of polled Friesian cattle. The farmhouse at Weston had five bedrooms, but his growing household now included his own six children, so he was looking for a new house as well as a new farm. He bought Letton for £38,000, but it was to be almost exactly a year before the family could move into the house.

There was a great deal of red tape involved in negotiating the purchase and its release from the Ministry of Defence. Mr Albert Bailey who had worked for the Eglingtons at Weston Longville and elsewhere, arrived some three weeks after the family, to take up the post of estate secretary. He remembers the situation well.

'When it was finally released by the MOD, the Hall and all the out-buildings were really in a very sorry state. The heating boilers in the basement, both domestic and central, were out of commission, as was the Power-House. Interior decorators and electricians were involved for quite a long period, in order to reinstate the indoor accommodation. Outside, our own staff took many weeks to rescue, repair and reinstate the iron railing round the semicircular front drive, which had been simply driven over, flattened and wrecked by the motor vehicles of various sections of HM forces in occupation…' [4]

Despite the daunting prospect, the family moved in and set about the task in hand. The children of George Eglington and his wife Elizabeth (Lizzie) were now growing or grown-up – Beryl was 22, Pearl 21, Ruby 20, Derek, the only boy, 17, Catherine 12 and Anna seven – but for the first time in their family life everyone could have a room of their own (**10:2**). They kept 12 bedrooms furnished, and from the entries in their Visitors' Book it seems if they were often full with guests as well as family. Over the span of a few years, visitors from more than 20 different countries signed in, staying from just one night to six months or more…They included not only family friends but farm students and exchange students.

One interesting visitor was a M. Suain from Belgian, who stayed for several months in 1948. The children noticed that he was often climbing up the Letton water tower seeming to enjoy sitting on the top having his lunch or enjoying the view, and they asked him why. It seemed that he worked in the Resistance during the war and evaded capture by living in a disused water tower where he could sleep and eat undetected. The Letton Tower just made him 'feel at home'.

10:2 Letton was truly a family house for the Eglingtons. Standing: Beryl, Auntie Dora, Pearl. Seated: Ruby, Catherine, George, Elizabeth, Anna, Derek

PHOTOGRAPH COURTESY OF THE EGLINGTON FAMILY

As well as the guests of the family, there were other visitors immediately post–war who left their mark. On Shipdham Airfield there was a German prisoner-of-war camp and six men were detailed-off to live and work at Letton as labourers on the estate. They are remembered arriving in an armoured van and marching into the kitchen courtyard with an impressive clatter of boots. They were billeted in what used to be the Male Servants Wing and in part of the Hall cellars, with five men working full time and the sixth finishing at mid day to cook for the others. One of them, who seemed a stereotype of 'the enemy army', was upsetting the others and was taken away early on. The others stayed, getting on well with the household and in some cases moving out into the village community as well.

Daphne, the Baileys' ten-year-old daughter, recalls them with the clarity of childhood memory:

> 'They were extremely kind to me. At Christmas they always came to spend an evening with us, and I played the piano and we all sang carols. They taught me three verses of 'Stille Nacht'. Matthias was almost sixty years old; he spoke no English and always seemed very unhappy and defeated. Nicklaus (or Nicki) was their cook and always came home from work early to make the evening meal – and occasionally I was invited. He was a very clever toy maker and made me several little toys from wood. Karl was the most distant and with his 'pebble-specs' and shaven head he seemed the most foreign to me. Helmut was younger and dark and spoke good English. Ernst (Ernie) was young too and spoke English, but was blond with blue eyes. He was an extremely good footballer and as time went on, he played for both Cranworth and then for Shipdham (a much better team!)'.

For more than 40 years after the event there was a label tacked onto the heavy door to the wine cellar, just below a cell-like window, which had typed on it the name 'Cpl. Müller'. What a cause for speculation! Was a German POW locked in there, in a kind of prison cell? But from the sound of them all, as described by Daphne, it was more likely that he found it merely a cool spot to sleep, during the summer. Perhaps even, he was the one who knew about wines and felt at home amidst racks for 1,500 bottles – even if they were all empty.

One of these men didn't return home at the end of their time at Letton, but stayed on and found work locally as a cowman. When one strips away the label 'Prisoner-of-War', it is interesting to consider their situation as individuals, struggling like other people on the estate to bring life back under control after the disruption of war. It is possible that the one who stayed had lost all his family in the war and no longer had any ties left in Germany, so felt he could settle in England happily. The war put enormously heavy pressure on families.

It is interesting, too, to consider the impact on younger members of the local community, even on the household of Letton with its several unattached young ladies, when a blond blue-eyed athlete arrived. One of the fascinating by-products of war in the area was the arrival of US Airforce men, Land Army girls and German POWs. At least two men on the estate married Land Army girls: Syd Banham who married Dot, and Kenny Graves who married Ethel.

CHANGES

One group of people who don't appear in the post-war household are the servants. Until 1939 there had been eight or ten full-time indoor staff, but apart from two or three ladies who came in daily to help with some of the cleaning and washing, there was now no one. Mrs Lizzie Eglington had her old school friend, Dorothea Greenwood – 'Auntie Dora' to the family – living with them and in theory they split the work between them; Mrs Eglington did the cleaning and Auntie Dora did the cooking, but it seemed a fairly flexible arrangement particularly as Dorothea Greenwood was slightly disabled.

What had changed? The house hadn't got any smaller, and by all accounts, the hospitality offered to guests hadn't reduced either. But no doubt there was less formality about the entertaining, and more help from both family and guests in running the house; and a general change in expectations on the part of everyone involved. Perhaps labour-saving devices really did save labour. But it seems nevertheless a remarkable change of circumstances.

There were several other changes slowly beginning to emerge as the Letton estate went from being one of around 5,000 acres to one of 1,000 acres. Letton Hall itself changed from being a Country Seat to being a working family farmhouse, and changes associated with this were to accelerate during the Eglingtons' time. There was also something else, though, that had already happened in the background without much publicity but which presaged radical changes.

A NEW SUCCESSION SYSTEM

Up to the early part of the 20th century, the principle of the eldest son inheriting the estate was a cherished and hard-fought concept. It would probably have continued for longer if the Gordons had had children or the war had not intervened. But as it was, succession became task- or organisation-orientated, rather than birth based.

When Arthur Gordon transferred the property to the Bradford Property Trust in the early part of the war, there was suddenly no Squire; no one to touch the cap to, no one whom everybody knew *wanted things done this way or that*. There was of course a legal owner, but no one single high-profile person in charge. When the Army took over, the situation must have been even more unclear, with the occupying military units following their own new priorities with very little knowledge or regard for the running of the house and gardens, or for its interdependence with the agricultural estate.

What seems to have happened is that the succession fell to those who had been carrying out the tasks under Squire Gordon, and who continued them through the Bradford Trust and Army period. In some cases, they continued on into the Eglingtons' era.

The Banham and Thetford families are examples of this; Harry Banham had been farm bailiff for Mr Gordon, and remained in that role until well after the war. He was still on the payroll in 1950; and even after that time he maintained his influence, since his daughter married Donny Thetford who was George Eglington's farm foreman and right-hand man for many years. In fact Donny continued as foreman for a while working for Chris Eglington, George's grandson. An impressive 'succession' record.

Mr Jack Tuddenham was the estate carpenter and general maintenance man from the mid-thirties up until the fifties, once again spanning three owners, plus the Army as occupiers. He was a skilled woodworker, able to turn his hand to all the many carpentry and building jobs around the estate. He lived in one of the Park Cottages and is remembered as a kind and gentlemanly person, married but with no children; an approachable friend to all the young people on the estate.

Mr Wally Fawkes the blacksmith lived in Shipdham, but had his own blacksmith's shop and forge in the Northhill buildings. Daphne remembers helping him as 'a good bellows-blower for the fires!'

Mr Marsh was the head gardener, and lived in Gardeners Cottage on the estate, until his death. In Mr Gordon's time, the walled kitchen garden was remembered as growing peaches, nectarines and apricots, plus many other exotics, many of them named with lead tags nailed to the walls near where they grew. There was also a melon pit and a mushroom house. From the sale particulars of September 1944 it is clear Mr Marsh had kept up the work through the war time for it is described as, '*a Walled-in Market Garden in high state of cultivation containing a Vinery, Peach House, Mushroom House, Potting Shed and Carnation House*'.[5]

It was to these men and their families, assisted no doubt by others whose names don't show so clearly in the records, that a kind of 'second level of succession' passed. With no obvious Squire, it was to them that the responsibility must have fallen for maintaining standards and priorities, and for retaining the working knowledge of the house and estate so necessary for its efficient operation; they kept the life and work of Letton going.

When Mr George Eglington took over in 1945, he was firmly in charge of course but it seems that now the succession-links had once been broken, the chain was never going to be unbreakable again. The concept of a large house set in the midst of its own estate, passed down from one generation to another was no longer to exist. Economic and political factors had speeded up this process, but regardless of any new succession system, the agricultural life of Letton went on from strength to strength.

MR GEORGE EGLINGTON, FARMER

Mr George Eglington (**10:3**) was 'an outstanding figure in the agricultural world' said the *Eastern Daily Press* in May 1976. [6] He built on the experience and reputation he had gained before coming to Letton, and before long the new 1,000-acre farm was running well with a team of around 30 people on the books.

He had started his farming successes with Welsh pigs, breeding them with three imported Swedish Landrace pigs and by the time he came to Letton he was well established as a leading pig farmer. He was modest about his achievements, though, recognising the help of his father and saying 'I was given some out-buildings that were not needed, and with beginner's luck I made a profit from my first pigs.' [7] He became President of the Welsh Pig Society and was

10:3 Mr George Eglington. PHOTOGRAPH COURTESY OF THE EGLINGTON FAMILY

known as *'the father of the improved Welsh breed'* [8], with his pigs taking main show awards all over the country including six breed championships at the 'Royal'. By 1963 the Letton herd was the largest in the country, but he decided to sell. At the age of 62, he said 'I don't want to retire – but nor do I want too many things to do.' [9]

He certainly didn't leave himself with nothing to do. Instead he merely wanted more time for his other major interest; the development of polled Friesian cattle. He felt that with too many irons in the fire, something had to go, and had decided it must be the pigs, because they had 'got there' whereas the cattle had not. [10]

He had first become interested in polled cattle when, as a boy, he looked after a naturally-polled black and white cow and noticed that it was an extraordinarily good milker and bred regularly. [11] Ten years before coming to Letton, he discussed this with Sir John Hammond, the internationally known geneticist and livestock expert, and as a result he embarked on a breeding programme to take the horns off his herd. In the early 1960s a Polled Friesian Herd Book was established in which only pure polled bulls which had been tested on 12 horned cows and produced horn-less calves were registered. A Polled Friesian Cattle Society was set up, and in 1963 George Eglington was recorded as Chairman. Around the same time, the English Jersey Cattle Society started discussions about a separate register for polled Jerseys, noting the work carried out by Mr Eglington, who by then had perhaps the greatest number of polled Jerseys in the country *'a dozen or so each of bulls and heifers'* [12].

As well as his direct farming interests, George Eglington found time to pursue his great hobby of coursing and at one time had twenty greyhounds, and won many trophies including the Waterloo Cup. He also had a particular interest in helping and encouraging young farmers and was active on the committees of the Young Farmers Clubs of both Reepham and Dereham. Several of his students (from the Norfolk School of Agriculture, now Easton College) would stay at Letton for six months or so while they were gaining experience on the farm. One of these students wrote in a letter 'I gained vast experience from Mr Eglington's knowledge…he was a man ahead of his time, and I look back with affection on what he achieved' [13]. In a different age bracket, another visitor wrote in the Visitors' Book – in a child's handwriting – 'the best holiday I've had and I have learnt a lot about farming thanks to Mr Eglington… I've never tasted such lovely strawberries and cream'.

The vicar of Cranworth, Canon Edward Bardwell, remembers George Eglington as a man of very likeable personality, of unfailing courtesy and kindness; a father figure in the community and a man of just and upright feelings. But he also suspected him (rather disapprovingly, one feels) of harbouring a liking for the rascally rogue, whether in mischievous young boys, or in animals – and quotes his 'poacher's dog', the lurcher Badger, as an example of this. [14]

There's no doubt that George Eglington had a good sense of humour even if a rather dry one. Towards the end of his life, he was admitted to the Norfolk and Norwich hospital for check-ups following a collapse and blackout. The doctor, checking his condition, said 'Who's this?'

'That's my wife.'

'And this?'

'That's my daughter, Ruby', he replied.

'And who is on the throne of England?'

'Well, when I came in it was Queen Elizabeth', said George, 'but I'm not sure who it is now!'

He also enjoyed gently teasing any tradesman or contractor that wanted his order by suggesting they had to beat him at table-tennis; there was a table permanently set up in the basement of the Hall and not many people were able to beat a well-practised Mr Eglington. He meted out the same treatment to his farm students, and invited them in for a game and a drink – but if they expected a generous gin and tonic, they were disappointed; it was always a blackcurrant juice or something similarly non-alcoholic.

EGLINGTON FAMILY LIFE

Letton Hall was very much a family house for all the Eglingtons. Christmas times around a vast table in the Dining Room were particularly special occasions, and often friends were invited home to share the hospitable atmosphere. But it wasn't long after arriving that various members of the family started to flee the nest. Pearl married Sam Marriage, from the flour milling family in Essex in December 1946 in the Friends Meeting House in Norwich. The reception was held at the Hall, and as one wit wrote in the Visitors' Book *'when cowman's daughter marries a miller's son – it's some eats!'*

Daughter Beryl left to pursue an overseas teaching career, and in July 1949 Ruby married Eric Wright. They were to set up home for a few years in a flat created for them around the kitchen courtyard, and Ruby's presence 'on the spot' for this time helped her to be involved in the running of the farm. Although she lived at Letton only until 1952, she continued an important role for most of the next 30 years or so.

The farming gene had affected other daughters in the family and in her early 20s Catherine produced a comprehensive and accomplished 50-page study of a year on the farm.[15]

Derek married his wife Sybil in 1953, having completed a course at the Royal Agricultural College, and his father set him up with the 200-acre Gurdon farm. At the start of his training,

10:6 Four generations of Eglingtons, gathered outside Letton's front door – Samuel, a young Christopher, his father Derek, and Mr George Eglington.

PHOTOGRAPH COURTESY OF THE EGLINGTON FAMILY

Derek had been reluctant to go into farming being more of an engineer at heart; but he was the only son of a farmer with five daughters – with a lot of expectation riding on that – and having made the commitment stuck to it. From then on his main preoccupation was running Gurdon Farm which was separate from the remaining 800 acres of the estate. This latter was run as a company – S. S. Eglington and Son Ltd. – so when the time came for succession considerations, the chain had been broken and it was no longer a simple matter of primogeniture.

HANDING ON THE HALL

The Eglington family were noted for living a long time, so it was understandable that George Eglington didn't feel any great sense of urgency in making succession plans despite a couple of health warnings in his early seventies. However he was at last persuaded that it was in the interests of both the farm and the family to think about the future.

His main priority was the continuance of the agricultural estate without breaking up the acreage. But the various farmhouses, farm buildings and cottages were also a part of the picture – and of course in the centre of it all stood Letton Hall.

A hundred years ago, the Hall was the focus of a 5,000-acre community with several hundred people looking to it for their livelihoods and those of their children – and even to some extent their lifestyle. Now, with the reducing number of people employed on the land, and the reduced size of the estate itself, the presence of the hall was no longer so relevant. It had served the Eglingtons well as a family house, but 30 years after their original arrival, most of the family had moved away. In practical terms, the house was much too big for its role.

Also, in practical terms proper maintenance and upkeep needed many more resources than could be justified for a family home – and for a reducing family at that. Any family house requires maintenance of course but the sheer size of a house like Letton is what absorbed extra resources, with labour and material costs all increased several-fold. The skilled tradesmen needed for the upkeep of an old house, especially one which is architecturally important, become scarcer and more expensive as years go by.

But practical thoughts are not the only consideration when dealing with well-loved houses such as Letton, as is true with many similar houses of course. Emotional and social ties are very strong and will often outweigh practical concerns.

When George Eglington and his family drew up their plans for the future they included keeping the Hall and all the farms and cottages, as well as maintaining and developing the acreage of agricultural land. The mechanism for achieving this was to set up trusts so that the estate could be passed on without family dispute, and without paying excessive death duties. Mr Eglington, then just turned 70, had to live for at least a further seven years; but bearing in mind the longevity of most of his family, this didn't seem a problem. However things were not to work out as hoped for.

Not long after setting up the trusts, George Eglington walked down the Shipdham Drive as usual to collect the newspapers, but seemed to be a long time before returning. Someone went to investigate and found him collapsed by the fence, apparently having suffered some kind of a blackout; there were to be two of these attacks resulting in a short spell in hospital to investigate. Some precautionary measures were taken but otherwise life went on very much as before back at Letton, until Friday 8 May 1976. Ruby, visiting, found her father looking very poorly and she and her mother helped him to bed. In the morning Dr David Dickie the Shipdham GP visited and found him looking much better, protesting that it was all a lot of fuss about nothing. Dr Dickie was duly persuaded and set off on a short fishing holiday – but early on Sunday morning, George Eglington got out of bed saying 'Something very odd is happening to me', collapsed and died.

Apart from the sadness and grief of his large family, now numbering 15 grandchildren and two great-grandchildren, the timing of his death was bad news for the estate. Being only two and a half years into the seven years required for the trusts to operate fully, meant that there was a substantial sum due for Death Duties; something would have to be sold.

Land was not to be touched if at all possible; of the buildings that could be spared, one obvious one was the farmhouse belonging to Low Farm, so this was sold for refurbishment. But that still left the question of the Hall itself to be resolved, and there was still a large amount of money to be found. Opinions differed sharply within the family, but eventually the economics of the situation dictated the action to be taken, and it was decided to sell the Hall.

There was now only Mrs Lizzie Eglington living full-time in the main rooms with Beryl there from time to time and Catherine living in the courtyard flat with her two children. Many of the rooms were unused, and maintenance needs were beginning to show themselves. An earlier outbreak of dry rot had been dealt with but there were signs of further outbreaks; the sooner action was taken the better.

Ruby took the step of instructing Hubert Sheringham of Irelands, the Estate Agents, and set about what was to be more than a year's campaign to find a buyer. She developed two standard tours of the house for prospective purchasers – a two-hour and a three-hour-plus version. At least one visitor found the trek too much and had to come again the following day to complete it. The task was demanding for Ruby too, especially when there was more than one tour needed on the same day. There was one lighter moment though, when a visitor arrived by helicopter and although deciding not to buy, took Ruby and Mrs Eglington for his own airborne tour of the house and gardens.

At last, at the end of 1979 a purchaser was found, and on 1 December the Carroll family moved in. Letton Hall had now only ten acres of land, and the final, perhaps inevitable break had been made from its historic role of a mansion in the centre of its own substantial estate.

1   Pam Barnes, *Norfolk Landowners since 1880*, Centre of East Anglian Studies, University of East Anglia, 1993, p30ff.

2   Nikolaus Pevsner, *The Buildings of England – NW and S Norfolk*, 1962, illustration on page 62.

3   The full auction particulars are in the Norfolk Record Office, BR/143/184.

4   Mr Albert Bailey and his daughter Daphne have contributed valuable information and correspondence for this chapter. Details are held on file by the author.

5   As above, Norfolk Record Office BR 143/184.

6   *Eastern Daily Press*, Tuesday 11 May 1976, in an obituary.

7   Ibid.

8   Ibid.

9   *Eastern Daily Press*, 19 November 1963.

10 Ibid.

11 *Eastern Daily Press*, 26 January 1963.

12 *Eastern Daily Press*, 18 January 1961.

13 Mr Richard Masters – student 1962–3. The author has a copy of correspondence on file.

14 Cranworth and Southburgh Parish Bulletin, May – June 1976.

15 Catherine Eglington, *A Norfolk Farm Study 1954–5 – Letton Hall Farms*. Not published but the author holds a copy on file.

NEW HARVEST

THE AGRICULTURAL HARVEST CHANGES
TO A SPIRITUAL ONE

There was a significant time and date that lay behind the start of this new chapter in the life of Letton; it was 7.15am on Thursday 17 August 1978, but an explanation of its full significance must wait until the Personal Postscript to this book. At the time there was no inkling that events would lead Letton once again to change its future; and that the traditional agricultural harvest of the estate would become a spiritual one.

WHY COME TO LETTON?

The Carroll family (**11:1**) were living in Sussex and fully occupied in running a medium-sized family business, but in addition to this had a spare-time involvement with young peoples' groups in their local church and in other national Christian youth organisations. For groups like this time spent away on some kind of residential activity was very helpful and constructive for personal and group development; and there was a need for 'places to go'.

In the summer of 1979 the Carrolls visited Letton Hall as a family, armed with the sale details, to see if they liked the house. An appointment had been arranged with Ruby Wright and she had asked whether the full tour was wanted or the shorter one. Politely the two-hour tour was requested although privately the view was that having been round so many houses over previous months it would be finished in half an hour or an hour at the most. More than three hours later the family got back into the car, footsore and tired, said the goodbyes, waited until Ruby was out of sight – and burst into laughter.

A house larger than the one in Sussex was needed to set up what was planned but Letton was ridiculous. It was far too big; the limit of the Carrolls' vision at that time was a comfortable farmhouse with perhaps a few extra bedrooms, and a barn or something similar alongside where a dozen or two bunk beds could be set up. So Letton was forgotten and the search continued around East Anglia, but the right property just didn't seem to be available.

In the meantime it was heard that Letton had been sold; then later that it hadn't been sold but had been taken off the market. It wasn't until some very determined purchaser of the Carrolls' house in Sussex insisted on an early exchange of contracts that the Carrolls wondered again about Letton. Then an unexpected phone call from Ruby set serious thoughts in motion; a decision was made, the formalities completed and the move in started on 1 December 1979.

It was yet another major change in the life of the Hall. It had been a mansion in the centre of its estate, it had been an Army HQ, it had been a large family farmhouse. Now it was something

11:1 The author and his wife Mary, with their family, just before moving to Letton.

entirely different once again; a permanent family home, but that home was in one of the servant's wings leaving the main Hall itself and the stable buildings for conference-centre-type accommodation.

COSTS AND ALTERNATIVE USES

It is interesting to look back at the history of the house and conclude that most major changes have been dictated by economic circumstances. This would seem to have been a major factor when the Gurdon family left the house after 130 years of ownership, as a result of changes in the agricultural scene. It was certainly the case when the Eglingtons decided to sell.

A house such as Letton needs people working full time to maintain it in condition; not to improve it, or to run a business from it, or support or serve a family – merely to look after the maintenance and administration of the house itself, and to stop it from deteriorating. On top of these direct wages, other costs for fuel and maintenance mount up before any business or family living costs are taken into account. To live in any kind of style, or to improve the house, increases this requirement substantially; in times of increasing pressure on expenditure, it becomes increasingly difficult to accept this extra cost.

11:2 This aerial view of Letton illustrates the idea of a 'pyramid of hierarchy' where a few people in the main hall (at the top of the picture) were supported by a 'pyramid' of servants and estate workers from the servants' wings, stables and outbuildings (lower down in the picture). Nowadays the situation is turned upside down.

On a large labour-intensive agricultural estate of 200 years ago it was relatively easy to absorb the costs, and to maintain a large household and luxurious lifestyle. Also, Mr and Mrs Gordon had resources gained from ship-owning to support their household. But on a reduced size of estate such as the Eglingtons', with pressure on costs and labour reduction, it was much more difficult; hence the search for alternative or additional uses, not just for Letton but for many country houses.

When the Carrolls moved in economic factors were still a major consideration. Costs needed to be kept low so that young people could afford to come, so this meant group self-catering, at least in the early days. Also some extra facilities had to be provided on site. The financial structure set up was a registered charitable trust, the *Letton Hall Trust*, with a non-denominational Christian basis, to operate and maintain the centre. In this way the non-profit making aims of the project were emphasised and any financial benefits available to charities could be sought by the trust. Ownership of Letton remained with the Carrolls, thereby avoiding the need for the Trust to raise a large capital sum; the property was leased to the Trust at a rent of no more than the open market figure.

An official '*Alternative Use*' for Letton had now been set up. In order to meet the running costs of large houses, and thus preserve them, organisations such as SAVE Britain's Heritage or the Society for Preservation of Ancient Buildings encourage the search for alternative uses; and to highlight this aim they publish books and leaflets with such ominous titles as *The Destruction of the Country House* or *The Country House: to be or not to be* [1]. A major achievement was for Letton to appear in the 1983 publication *Vanishing Houses of England* under the heading 'Houses Saved and Adapted to New Uses' [2]. Success!

Cost-saving meant that wages were kept to a minimum and a great deal of work was carried out by volunteers. Some arrived for a weekend working party, but others formed a resident team of 'Lettoneers' staying for several months or even longer, often young people between university and career, or adults with some time available.

Out of this new situation came the concept of an 'upside-down hierarchy'; an aerial view of the house and servants' quarters demonstrates this pictorially (**11:2**). For most of the life of Letton there had been a pyramid of support for the family living in the Hall, with perhaps 10 indoor servants plus another 10–15 working in the stables and gardens, with an estate staff of 200 outside. Now the pyramid was turned completely upside down with a 'family' of six or eight caring for up to 150 visitors.

FAMILY EVENTS

In the midst of the early stages of work, just six months after moving into Letton, Mary Carroll fell suddenly ill, and 40 days later died of an aggressive cancer; it was entirely unexpected, and caused enormous grief. A letter came to light recently which was sent to friends at the time:

It is with sadness I write… as we come to terms with the gaps that Mary's death leaves… Her children Jonathan, Simon and Bridget were returning to school and university and the letter went on to say, *I am not looking forward to living alone in the family flat, during the autumn term.*

From the Letton project a housekeeper, policy-maker, bookings-administrator, secretary, bookkeeper and 'getter-of-things-done' had been lost. Mary at 42 became the third of the '*Mistresses of Letton*' to die relatively young, and sharing in the poignancy of those previous deaths somehow helped the author to come to terms with Mary's death; the house had witnessed these things before – involving other Marys too – and its continued solid existence was somehow a comfort.

During Mary's time in hospital she had met Kay Nundy who was one of the nurses from whom she had received special care. Kay had offered to help Mary through some convalescent nursing a few weeks ahead, when it was expected that she would be coming out of hospital, but when that date came Mary had already died. Kay nevertheless came and helped with the Letton household for several weeks as a 'Lettoneer', and helped care for the family.

Nearly two years later, after another of Letton's love stories Kay and the author were married, and he became the fourth owner to enter into a second marriage – and also one of those three who had an average age difference of more than 20 years between husband and wife. When Jenny, Rachel and Ben were born, the tradition was continued of at least some of Letton's owners having a family of six children or more (**11:3**). It must be something to do with a sense of responsibility for having so many rooms to fill.

ADAPTING THE HOUSE

As had always happened in the past, the working life of Letton had to continue despite the demands of family situations. In this current era the work involved adapting the house to accommodate visiting groups of up to 150 people.

11:3 The author and his wife Kay, with their family who were all born during the early years of the Letton project – although in this picture they appear to be looking back to an even earlier age.

Could the house adapt to such extremes? Could it be made to work? The answer was yes. The house was, after all, designed from the beginning to be a place of leisure and pleasure; John Soane's original floor plans provided rooms for eating and meeting and socialising – with perhaps a little serious study in the library; but there were virtually no 'business rooms'. Fascinatingly these are almost precisely the requirements of a youth conference, or church weekend away; country house parties had been held at Letton for many decades and continuing them seemed a natural practice. Some of the details were not of course what John Soane may have envisaged, but this is a reflection of the changes in lifestyle over the years; one feels that somehow Soane would not have disapproved.

When the house is full of visitors it is good to walk around outside after dark; the lights are on and the house is outlined against the sky. Strolling along the paths one can see, through the lighted windows of the Dining Room and Drawing Room, people enjoying the house so much. The house works in a wonderful way as a living space for people, which is surely the greatest success an architect can achieve.

However, beneath the veneer of the traditional house-parties of previous decades, some changes have had to be made. A comparison which brings these to mind is to see the difference between the old Dining Room and the new. One picture (**11:4**) shows it around 1910 laid for three people; one can imagine the soft chink of glass and cutlery, as white-gloved footmen bring in silver tureens. The other picture (**11:5**) shows it as it was more recently, ready to be invaded by 60 or 80 teenagers straight in from football on the field, all talking enthusiastically at the same time, wanting feeding *now*!

At all times it was sought to make the changes to the main hall reversible; the hall itself is listed as Grade II* and its important architectural features needed to be preserved. But at the same time the dry-rot infestation that had taken hold in a number of areas of the building needed to be dealt with decisively. Also, toilets and bathroom areas needed to be up-graded; visitors were fascinated to hear that John Soane had only felt it necessary to provide one WC but they considered progress should have been made since then. The Victorians, and after them Arthur Gordon, had of course improved on Soane's facilities, but more needed to be done.

The stables were an area which needed major adaptation. They had begun with eighteenth-century grandeur, incorporating carriage houses, washing down areas and extensive tackrooms and haylofts, and had already accepted well the changes needed for the motoring age with workshops and motor-houses. During the war they were a military base, and after that a multi-purpose farmyard; but in the end they adapted very well to be sleeping, meeting and eating accommodation for up to 50 or 60 young people. Sometimes it was tempting to keep the changes to a minimum, such as adapting the wall-mounted feeding troughs for horses that ran along the full length of one wing, to be a feeding trough for teenagers – but the temptation had to resisted and the troughs had to go eventually.

One of the youth organisations that had been involved with the project from the start was West Runton Camps who, among other activities, operated go-karting camps. These had had to take place for several years on whatever Norfolk airfield the MoD was prepared to make available each summer; this arrangement was not completely satisfactory and the Kart Camps needed a permanent base. This was one of the priorities for the new life of Letton – fast and noisy and oily, not at all the kind of thing normally associated with a country house garden. But the volunteer work parties set to and cleared the abandoned area that had once been the gardeners' domain, and a kart-track was laid, weaving around the concrete bases where the RASC had built their Nissen huts.

The track was 400 m long and included pits and challenging corners; it was a dramatic trans-formation from 19-century pleasure grounds but it seemed to work, and even Edward Boardman's beautifully-built earth closets were pressed into service as a Technical Control Centre.

11:4 The Dining Room in 1913, laid out for Lord Cranworth and a few family members. This picture is from the Auction Particulars of 1913. (See Appendix II)

11:5 Here the same Dining Room is ready to receive a large group of teenage visitors.

The walled garden had not been kept up and needed ploughing over and re-seeded to provide an activities area; everywhere there was work to be done. News of the project spread and work parties and volunteers came from friends and family, and churches and youth groups from both locally and far afield. The tradition started of sending regular reports and newsletters out to all those involved in helping support Letton Hall Trust. A page from Report Number 4 (**11:6**) is shown with a definite sense of life at Letton 'being in a battle'. There's even a 'field kitchen' reported, set up in the Drawing Room. What *would* previous owners have made of that… Undoubtedly in the bustle of it all, a few things were done that shouldn't have been, or something was overlooked; jobs that have been regretted subsequently. But overall tremendous progress was made and the adaptation was a success.

11:6 An early edition of Letton News, reporting on the progress of the work.

Several of the Eglington family, still close enough neighbours to know what was going on, held their breath, but saw that the right sort of results were coming eventually. It is difficult to hand on the torch when someone takes over your old home, but they have always been most supportive and on several occasions the family has given, or directed, generous donations towards Letton Hall Trust. Also there have been a number of Eglington family occasions held at Letton, which have maintained a warm and helpful relationship. Lord Cranworth too, representing the Gurdon family, has always shown a supportive interest in the new custodians of his family home; and Sir John Soane's Museum has always gone out of its way to help us in our task.

HANDING ON THE HOUSE AGAIN

In February 2007 there came yet another key change in the life of Letton Hall; it was handed on once again.

Two years before this the Letton Hall Trust had marked 25 years of successful operation as a residential conference and activities centre and could be proud of its record. Each year more than 100 groups had visited including schools, colleges and universities as well as youth organisations and churches, and the visitors now regularly included overseas groups as well as people from all over the United Kingdom. There had been many big events as well, including weddings, family celebrations and even a few balls; more than 75,000 people had visited and enjoyed 'life at Letton'. Twenty-five volumes of Visitors' Books bore testimony to enjoyable and worthwhile times spent, sometimes with deep and life-changing moments.

Somehow this house which had seen political and public service, in both war-time and peace, and had offered country hospitality and agricultural progress, had now worked its influence over this new harvest.

The Carroll family had been pleased to make it their home and, as throughout the life of the house, there had been both love and loss; but while ownership remained with the family there was always the concern that the work of the Letton Hall Trust might be threatened through changes in family circumstances. The financial resources of the trust had gradually improved and finally in 2007 a sale was concluded.

It had been 270 years since Dillingham Brampton Gurdon had been born; 220 years since the Gurdon family had moved into the 'new' Letton Hall; now a new chapter had begun, but the life of Letton Hall continues.

1   Marcus Binney and Kit Martin, *The Country House: to be or not to be*, Save Britain's Heritage, London *c.* 1983.

2   Gervase Jackson-Stops, John Harris and Emma Milne, *Vanishing Houses of England*, Save Britain's Heritage and Jackson-Stops and Staff, London *c.* 1983.

APPENDIX I

MAPS

Maps can not only define a location but can also unlock the history, which makes some of the maps of Letton so interesting and helpful. They are not just directions but can tell stories and paint pictures. Working with them is part detective-work and part treasure-hunting but whenever the signs and clues on paper link up with those on the terrain there is a satisfying sense of achievement and orientation. There are a number of discrepancies in maps of different periods, but this is to be expected and provides opportunity for further study and fascinating 'puzzling over'.

References are given in the caption to each map but an overall acknowledgement needs to be given to two documents that provide authoritative and comprehensive comments in much more detail than it is possible to include here.

• Alan Davison *et al. Six Deserted Villages in Norfolk* East Anglian Archaeology Report No. 44, 1988, from the Archaeological Unit of the Norfolk Museums Service, provides a wealth of detail from the early history of Letton. Material from this publication is reproduced by courtesy of the Historic Environment Service, Norfolk County Council.

• Anthea Taigel and an MSC team, *A History of Letton Park* 1990, unpublished, Centre of East Anglian Studies, University of East Anglia, draws on the results of a field survey and continues with details up to the present day. Extracts and maps are reproduced with the permission of the Centre of East Anglian Studies, UEA.

LIST OF MAPS

1. An aerial photograph showing the remains of medieval Letton.
2. An interpretive map relating these remains to the present terrain.
3. A sketch map of the Letton estate in 1783, based on Isaac Lenny's map.
4. Road Order Map of 1783.
5. Road Order Map of 1791.
6. An extract from William Faden's Map of Norfolk, 1797.
7. The 1838 Tithe Award Map.
8. An interpretive sketch map relating to the 1838 Tithe Map.
9. An extract from the OS 6 inches to 1 mile map of 1959.

Map 1 Although this aerial photograph, taken by the RAF in 1946, is not a map in the strictest sense it shows up details of the early village of Letton very clearly. The remains of the church are visible in the lower right corner of the photograph; the 'hollow way' running from the church westwards towards a village pond can still be seen on the present terrain.

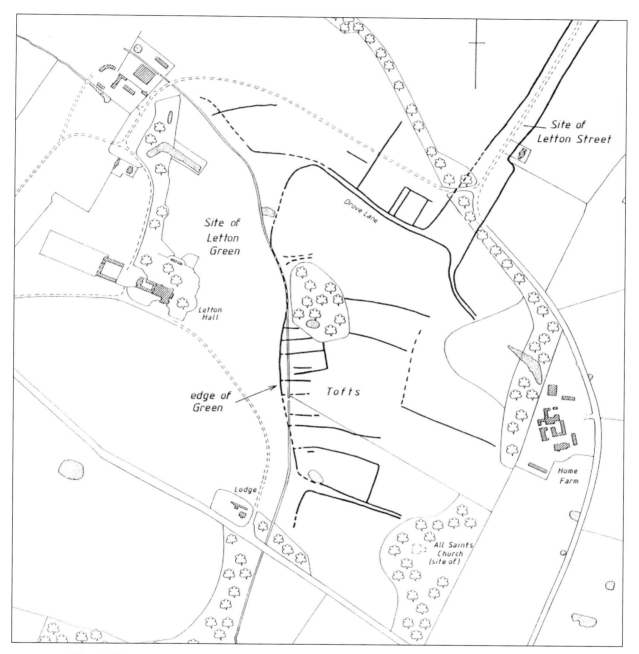

Map 2 This interpretive map identifies the features on the photograph and links them with the present terrain. From the position of the house platforms it can be seen that the village followed the line of the stream running north-south, and included at least two ponds. It is possible that the Lodge building was once part of the village, but no other buildings have survived.

THIS MAP IS REPRODUCED FROM EAA REPORT 44 WHICH CONTAINS A WEALTH OF DETAILED INFORMATION (SEE ACKNOWLEDGEMENT AND REFERENCES ABOVE).

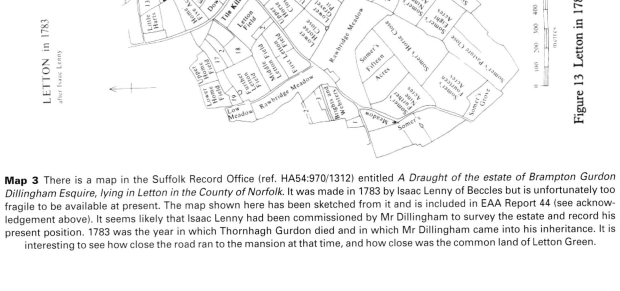

1 Meadow
2 Glebe
3 Grove
4 House and Yards
5 Barn Meadow
6 Lower Barn Meadow
7 Lane Pightle
8 Calves Pightle
9 Stacy
10 Garden Pightle
11 Two Acre Pightle
12 Mr Partridge's Land
13 Harts Pightle
14 Cows Pightle
15 Corams Meadow
16 Second Colly's Pightle
17 Long four acres
18 Wronglands
19 Little Meadow
20 Driftway
21 Brick Kiln Piece

Features superimposed soon after survey
—— Extent of Park
==== New roads

LETTON in 1783
after Isaac Lenny

Figure 13 Letton in 1783, based on Isaac Lenny's estate map. Scale 1:20,000. *(Published by kind permission of the Suffolk Record Office)*

Map 3 There is a map in the Suffolk Record Office (ref. HA54:970/1312) entitled *A Draught of the estate of Brampton Gurdon Dillingham Esquire, lying in Letton in the County of Norfolk*. It was made in 1783 by Isaac Lenny of Beccles but is unfortunately too fragile to be available at present. The map shown here has been sketched from it and is included in EAA Report 44 (see acknowledgement above). It seems likely that Isaac Lenny had been commissioned by Mr Dillingham to survey the estate and record his present position. 1783 was the year in which Thornhagh Gurdon died and in which Mr Dillingham came into his inheritance. It is interesting to see how close the road ran to the mansion at that time, and how close was the common land of Letton Green.

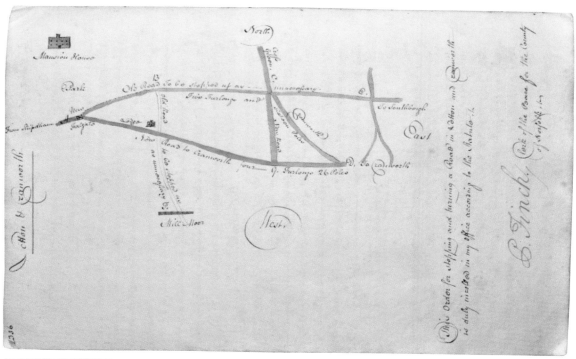

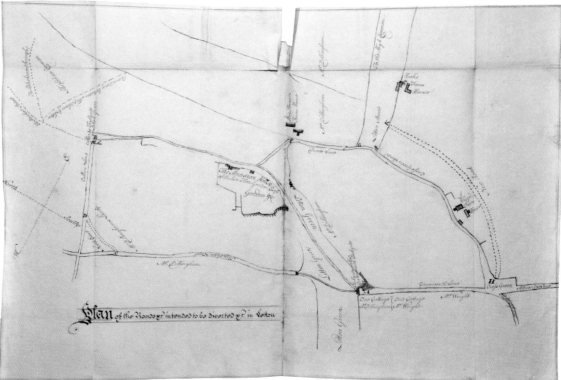

Maps 4 and 5 These two maps show intended road relocations within the Letton estate and are from the appropriate Road Order Books containing the text of the legal agreements; they are reproduced by permission of the Norfolk Record Office. No Parliamentary Act was required to carry this out as the Gurdons were the sole landowners in the parish at this time. The earlier map (NRO S/Cse 1 Road Order Book 1, 499 – 504) is dated 1783 and shows the roads to be closed in green. The later one (NRO S/Cse 1 Road Order Book 3, 332 – 36) is dated 1791 and shows a new road to the east of the mansion. Dr Tom Williamson in his *Archaeology of the Landscape Park* (BAR British Series 268, 1998) states that 'this is one of relatively few examples of settlement clearance associated with emparking in 18th-century Norfolk'

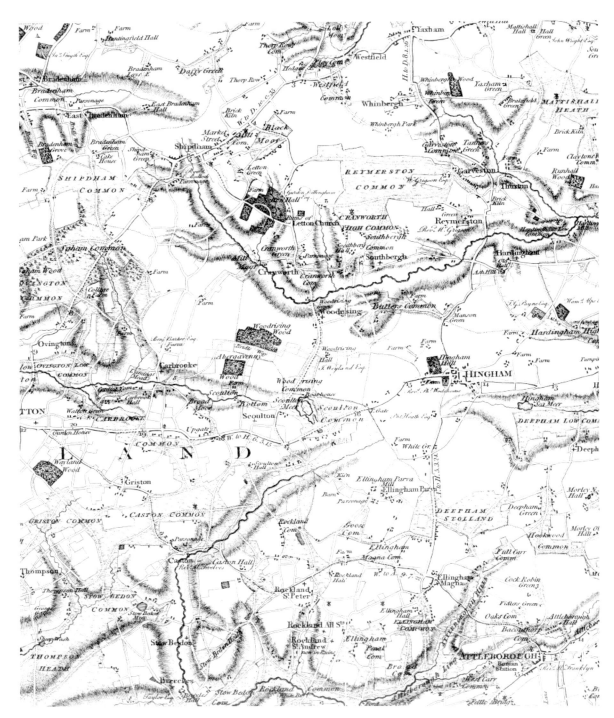

Map 6 William Faden's *Map of Norfolk*, 1797. This extract is from the first comprehensive surveyed map of Norfolk at a scale of 1inch to 1 mile, with an attempt to give an impression of relief and contours. It was a remarkable achievement by Faden 'Geographer to King George III and the Prince of Wales', after five years spent surveying, and published just 20 years after Mostyn Armstrong had tried and failed to complete a similar project.

REPRODUCED WITH PERMISSION FROM THE NORFOLK RECORD SOCIETY'S EDITION, 1973

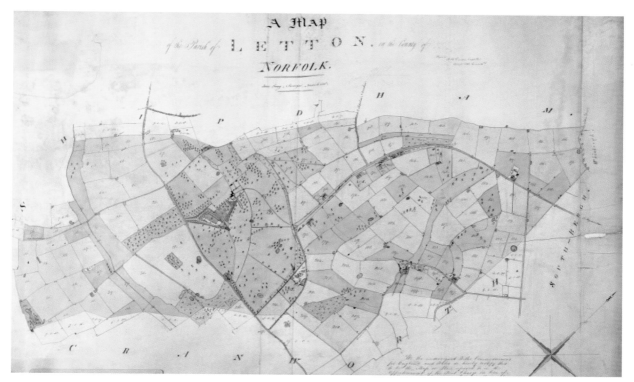

Map 7 The Tithe Map of 1838. Tithe maps of most of Norfolk were produced for the Tithe Commissioners in accordance with the Tithe Commutation Act of 1836, which required that payments to the church in the form of farm produce should be replaced by a money payment. It is interesting that the map for Letton was produced by one Isaac Lenny of Norwich – who would seem almost certain to be linked with the surveyor of Map 3, except that they are separated by at least 55 years. The most likely solution would appear to be that the first Isaac Lenny's son, born in 1793, carried on his father's profession.

REPRODUCED BY COURTESY OF THE NORFOLK RECORD OFFICE (NRO 79)

1 HALL, OFFICES, YARDS AND PLEASURE GROUND
2 GARDEN (WALLED IN)
3 GARDEN (NOT WALLED IN)
4 THE ORCHARD
5 FARM YARD AND OUTBUILDINGS
6 LAWN
7 LAWN
8 LODGE PLANTATION (WOOD)
11 CHURCH CLOSE (PASTURE)
12 CHURCH CLUMP (WOOD)
13 LAYERS (PASTURE)
14 THE BELT PLANTATION
15 THE NORTH PLANTATION
16 BELT PLANTATION
17 SCALS PIGHTLE (PASTURE)
18 DOVE HOUSE PADDOCK (PASTURE)
20 AARONS PADDOCK (PASTURE)
21 PLANTATION
22 COZENS (ARABLE)
23 GRANARY PADDOCK (PASTURE)
19 PLANTATION
24 PASTURE

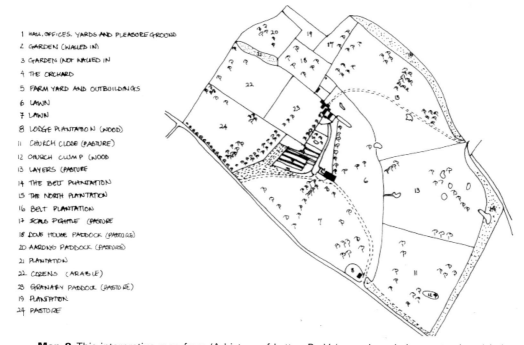

Map 8 This interpretive map from 'A history of Letton Park' (see acknowledgements above) helps to identify the various parcels of land include in the Tithe Map.

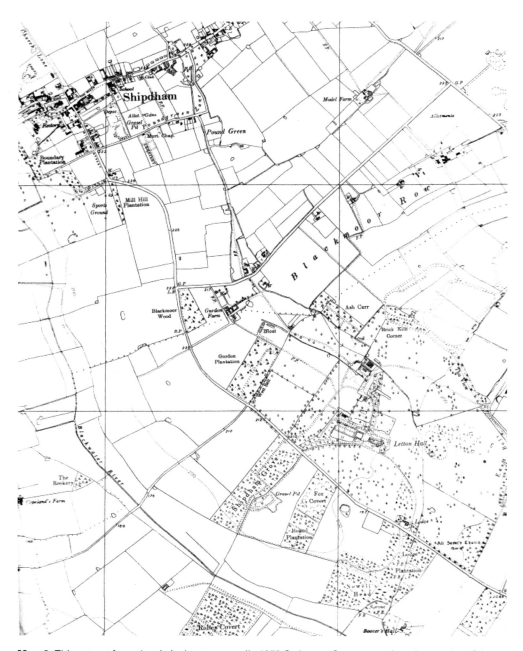

Map 9 This extract from the six inches to one mile 1959 Ordnance Survey map is a clear and useful map for present day needs – yet it has a long history. Boundaries were revised in 1950 but the map as a whole is marked as 'revised before 1930'. It is practically identical to the OS maps of 1884 and 1891 (respectively to the north and south of the main house) which in turn state they were both based on the survey of 1881–2.

Boardman's plans for the 'pleasure gardens' can be seen, as can the boomerang-shaped lake north of the hall which is accepted as the site of the old Letton Hall. The footbridge over this lake – presumably Boardman's bentwood design – is also marked. The spring to the south of the main hall, near Booters Hall, is shown but it is surprising that the Ice House is not marked, even on the 1884 map. This is to the SW of the hall half way down the wooded area marked Shipdham Grove, and must surely have been in existence in Sir John Soane's time.

APPENDIX II

Extracts from particulars of sale of the Letton Hall Estate – 3 October 1913.

Final Edition

By direction of
The Right Honourable Lord Cranworth

Letton Hall.
Norfolk.

Solicitors
Messrs. Frere Cholmeley & Co.
28 Lincolns Inn Fields, W.C.

Auctioneers
Messrs. Knight Frank & Rutley
20, Hanover Square
London, W.

A Brief Description of the Property.

The **Letton Hall Estate** is an attractive Residential, Agricultural and Sporting Property, situated 4 miles West of Thuxton Station on the Wymondham and Dereham Section of the Great Eastern Railway, 6 miles South-west from Dereham, 11 miles from Attleborough, 17 miles from Thetford, 17 miles from Norwich and 18 miles from Brandon. Post and Telegraph Office at Shipdham about 1½ miles.

Area by Ordnance Survey: 4,498 A. 2 R. 9 P.

Letton Hall, a substantial Mansion, stands in a finely-timbered Park of about 240 acres, with Two Entrance Drives, one having Lodge, and contains: Outer and Inner Halls, Dining Room, Drawing Room, Billiard Room, Study, 26 Bed and Dressing Rooms, Three Bathrooms, excellent Offices, capital Stabling for 16, with ample living accommodation. Good Water Supply, Petrol Air-gas Lighting, Modern Sanitation.

Beautiful Gardens and Grounds, including Italian Garden, Woodland Walks, Wild Garden and Ornamental Pools, Kitchen Gardens and Orchard. Gardener's House.

The Woodlands extend to about 141 acres and contain some well-grown Timber, and there are several new Plantations in thriving condition. The Hedgerow Timber is of considerable dimensions.

Shooting.—The Estate affords excellent Shooting, the Coverts being conveniently placed and capable of holding a considerable head of Game. The Partridge Ground is exceptionally good. The Bag for the last three seasons was as follows:—

Season	Pheasants	Part-ridges	Hares	Rabbits	Wood-cock	Snipe	Wild Fowl	Sundries	Total
1909-10 ...	1,800	370	138	916	7	42	4	991	4,268
1910-11 ...	1,989	317	210	1,117	9	25	28	153	3,848
1911-12 ...	4,465	1,107	216	635	16	29	23	58	6,549

Letton Hall, with the Shooting over the Estate, has been let until 1st February, 1914, at £900.

Hunting with the West Norfolk Foxhounds and the Norwich Staghounds.

3

A Brief Description of the Property—continued.

Agricultural.—The Estate is divided into some Thirty Farms and Small Holdings, of convenient size, with excellent Homesteads and generally in good repair, and let to practical Tenants at moderate Rents.

The Estate is famous for its Pedigree Herd of Red Poll Cattle, which may be acquired by a Purchaser by valuation if desired. The recent awards include: 15 Championships, 75 Firsts, 41 Seconds, 19 Thirds and other Honours to a total of 258.

Principal Seats in the Neighbourhood:—

Woodrising Hall: Walter Cubitt Crawshay, Esq.
Kimberley House: The Rt. Hon. The Earl of Kimberley, J.P.
Honingham Hall: The Rt. Hon. Sir Ailwyn Fellowes, K.C.V.O., D.L., J.P.
Hardingham Hall: Mrs. Edwards.
Reymerston Hall: Colonel Richard C. Hare, C.B.
Gressenhall House: Sir George R. L. Hare, Bart., D.L., J.P.
Merton Hall: The Rt. Hon. Lord Walsingham, D.L., J.P., LL.D., F.R.S.

Manors and Advowsons.—The Manors of Cranworth and Butler's in Letton, Booter's Hall in Cranworth and Reymerston Calvely Hall and the Advowsons of the Livings of Cranworth with Letton with Southburgh, Reymerston and Hackford will be included in the Sale of the whole Estate.

Rent Roll.—The actual Rental, and the estimated Rental of the Mansion, Sporting, Woods and Land in hand, amounts to

		£ s. d.
Actual	...	3,736 11 0
Estimated	...	1,171 12 0
		£4,908 3 0

Outgoings:—

		£ s. d.
Tithe Commutation Rent Charge, £984 8s. 9d. Value, 1913	...	735 15 7
Land Tax	...	165 8 3
Quit and Free Rents	...	14 10 7
Rates on Cottages	...	40 4 10
Total		£955 19 3

The Tithe Commutation Rent Charge and Land Tax will be informally apportioned by the Auctioneers to each Lot, and the respective amounts of such apportionments will be published in the Final Edition.

Tenure.—The Estate (with the exception of 204 A. 3 R. 1 P., which are Copyhold) is Freehold. See Condition of Sale No. 9.

4

Lots 4 to 43 (omitting Lot 24) inclusive will first be offered as a whole. See order of Sale, Page 5.

Lot 4.

(Coloured Brown on Plan.)

LETTON HALL

is approached by Two Drives through the finely timbered Park (one being guarded by a Brick built and Tiled Lodge), converging at the broad gravelled carriage sweep, surrounded by a Brick Balustrade.

The Mansion

was designed by the late Sir John Soane, and is substantially built of Brick with Stone Porch and Slated Roofs.

A pair of double doors open on to a flight of Stone steps, at the head of which another pair of glazed doors giving access to the

Entrance Hall,

measuring about 15 ft. 4 ins. by 13 ft., and leading through double doors to the

Inner Hall,

Oval in shape, and Ornamental Cornices, and lighted by a large Lantern Light.

On the right of the Entrance Hall is the

Billiard Room and Library,

measuring about 41 ft. 6 ins. by 19 ft. 4 ins., excluding a large Square Bay, Coved Ceiling and Ornamental Cornice. Hob Stove and White and Grey Marble Mantel, polished Oak Floor and Panelled Dado. Communicating is the

Drawing Room,

measuring about 30 ft. 4 ins. by 20 ft., lighted by three windows and having square recess at end about 14 ft. by 10 ft. 6 ins., polished Oak Floor, carved White Marble Mantel, Ornamental Cornice, windows opening on to Terrace. Double glazed doors lead to the

Conservatory,

with Tiled Floor and Stone Shelves.

Dining Room,

measuring about 32 ft. 4 ins. by 20 ft. 3 ins., with Steel Grate, Marble surround and carved Mantel, Ornamental Plaque Cornice, Oak Floor, Serving Lobby to back stairs.

12

A view of Letton Hall from across the park. Notice the conservatory opening off the Drawing Room.

Edward Boardman's bentwood bridge spanning the lake formed by what are presumed to be the foundations of the Old Hall.

Study,

measuring about 19 ft. 6 ins. by 15 ft. 6 ins., Marble Mantel, Coved Ceiling.

Lavatory (h. and c.), Two W.C's.

Side Hall with entrance to Garden.

The Principal Staircase

rises from the Hall and leads by an easy ascent to the Main Landing.

On the right is the GREEN BEDROOM, measuring 20 ft. by 19 ft. 6 ins., having three windows, and communicating with the GREEN DRESSING ROOM, measuring 15 ft. by 15 ft. 10 ins. The PRINCIPAL or BLUE BEDROOM, 20 ft. 6 ins. by 20 ft. 3 ins., facing South-east, with two windows and communicating with BATHROOM, fitted bath and W.C. The CANOPY BEDROOM, measuring 20 ft. 6 ins. by 12 ft. 4 ins. PASSAGE BEDROOM, measuring 16 ft. 9 ins. by 14 ft. 10 ins., fitted with cupboard. A Lobby from the back staircase leads to the RED BEDROOM, measuring 20 ft. 6 ins. by 19 ft. 3 ins. The PINK BEDROOM, measuring 14 ft. 8 ins. by 13 ft. 9 ins. BATHROOM with Bath. W.C. Housemaid's Cupboard. Sink (h. and c.). Approached by a separate staircase from the Garden Hall are a Bedroom, Lavatory and W.C., and another staircase leads to the Schoolroom and Bedroom adjoining.

On the Second Floor

WORKED ATTIC, measuring 20 ft. 6 ins. by 19 ft. BATHROOM, fitted Bath (h. and c.). The BROWN BEDROOM, measuring 19 ft. 2 ins. by 18 ft. 4 ins., fitted with Cupboard. The BROWN DRESSING ROOM, NIGHT NURSERY, measuring 19 ft. 4 ins. by 17 ft. 10 ins., with passage leading to DAY NURSERY, measuring 17 ft. 6 ins. by 15 ft. 9 ins. W.C. Housemaid's Cupboard.

The Servants' Accommodation

is in the Wing, and consists of Three Single and Four Double Bedrooms, Linen Cupboard, Store Cupboard and W.C. There are also Three Men's double Rooms.

The Domestic Offices

are in the Basement, and consist of: Servants' Hall, Pantry, Larder, large Kitchen with range and hot plate, Scullery, W.C., Housekeeper's Room, Store Cupboard, Wood Room, Cellar, Housemaids' Sitting Room, large Wine, Beer and other Cellars, Butler's Pantry, Strong Room, Footman's Bedroom, Box Room.

LUGGAGE LIFT TO ALL FLOORS.

13

Outside, with Paved Yard, are Meat Larder, Dairy, Boot Room, Game Larder, Gun Room, Coal-house, Bake-house.

WELL WITH WHEEL PUMP.

The WATER SUPPLY is derived from a Spring situated in Newell's Head Wood, No. 208 on Plan, Cranworth Parish.

The LIGHTING is by petrol air gas, generated in a Detached Building situated in the Orchard, No. 142 on Plan, Letton Parish.

The DRAINAGE was remodelled in 1909.

The Gardens and Grounds

surrounding the House are of simple design but of an attractive character. They consist of a broad Terrace Walk, Ornamental Lawns flanked with fine Copper Beech and other Trees and Rhododendrons.

Italian Garden,

with Sun Dial, and surrounded by Yew Trees. Flower Garden, Lawns, Ornamental Trees and Shrubs, Woodland Walks, Three Summer-houses. Two Ornamental Pools, one with Rustic Bridge. Evergreen Walk, leading to the Walled Kitchen and Fruit Gardens. Lean-to Vinery, Tomato House, Peach House, Bothy, Tool and Barrow Sheds, Second Kitchen Garden, another Lean-to Vinery, Three-division Lean-to Hot House with Pits, Cold Pits, Potting Shed, Two Pigsties, Drying Ground.

CAPITAL WELL-STOCKED ORCHARD.

GARDENER'S COTTAGE, Brick built and Slated, containing : Two Bedrooms, Two Sitting Rooms, Kitchen, Scullery, Larder. Wood Shed. Garden. Poultry House and Runs.

The Stabling

is built of Red Brick with Slated Roof, surmounted by a Clock Tower, is detached and encloses a large Paved Yard with Pump and Tank.

The Accommodation consists of :

Five Stalls, Loose Box, Three Stalls, Two Loose Boxes, Three Stalls, Harness Room, Two Stalls, Two Double Coach-houses, a larger Coach-house or Garage with Pit. Lofts.

MEN'S QUARTERS comprising : Sitting Room, Four Bedrooms, Kitchen, Store Room, Groom's Room.

14

A PERSONAL POSTSCRIPT

A key time and date for me is written on the flyleaf of the Bible I was reading at the time; it is '7.15 am, 17 August 1978'.

That morning, and for many mornings previously, as a Christian businessman I had been praying over the five-year plan for our family business – should we expand or consolidate, export more, manufacture more or import, and who should do what… but for some reason the future seemed to be unclear. Eventually, in frustration, I prayed a dangerous prayer, *Alright, Lord, what **do** you want me to do?*

In an instant a complete business-plan flashed into my mind, and I recognised it immediately as 'just right'. However, to my surprise I wasn't part of the company plan myself, apart from short term. It involved me taking a year to hand on the business to the people who had helped me in building it up – and from then on *there would be something else for me to do*. I felt that God had suddenly intervened in my life in a very direct way; it was quite unnerving were it not for the fact that with the plan came a sense of complete conviction that the course of action was correct. By noon that day I had implemented it within the company.

It took that year to implement the plan, and then almost a year later to the day, we visited Letton. Through a remarkable set of circumstances it became absolutely clear that Letton Hall was the right house to buy; and that same conviction saw us through all the difficulties that we encountered. Most important of all, my experience on that morning in August showed that God had initiated the project; the new chapter at Letton was going to be His work.

Since that time there have been pages and pages of Visitors' Books filled with signatures and comments, and many editions of *Letton News*; It is truly a Christian venture and the agricultural harvest of the original Letton Hall estate has been turned into a spiritual one. It would be good to include more in this book but there just isn't space… the Apostle John, at the end of his Gospel, said, 'Jesus did many other things as well. If every one of them was written down, I suppose that even the whole world would not have room for the books that would be written'. John 21; verse 25.

Perhaps, in that enormous pile of thrilling books, there will be the ongoing story of Letton Hall.

INDEX